GROWTH OF SCHEDULED TRIBES AND CASTES IN MEDIEVAL INDIA

By the same author :

History of the Khaljis, 1950, 1967, 1980
Twilight of the Sultanate, 1963, 1980
Studies in Medieval Indian History, 1966
Studies in Asian History (edited), 1969
Growth of Muslim Population in Medieval India, 1973
Early Muslims in India, 1984
The Mughal Harem, 1988
Indian Muslims: Who Are They, 1990, 1993
The Legacy of Muslim Rule In India, 1992
Muslim Slave System in Medieval India, 1994

Growth of Scheduled Tribes and Castes in Medieval India

K.S. LAL

ADITYA PRAKASHAN
NEW DELHI

First Published 1995

ISBN: 978-8-186-47103-6

Published by Voice of India, 2/18, Ansari Road, New Delhi – 110 002.
Printed at Replika Press Pvt. Ltd.

Preface

The Scheduled Castes, the Scheduled Tribes, the Dalits and the Other Backward Castes are there in large numbers in present-day India. Many backward classes were there from the pre-historic or very ancient times, many more were added in the medieval period spanning over a thousand years. Their numbers went on growing because of the conflicts of the times arising out of the policies of Muslim invaders and rulers. Contrary to modern-day make-believe, there is no evidence to show that the lower classes suffered from the tyranny of the Hindu upper classes in the medieval period. If it were true that the backward classes were so terribly oppressed by the Brahmanas, we would expect them to take some kind of revenge by making common cause with the Muslim persecutors of the Brahmanas. But exactly opposite is the case. Jats and Meds helped the Brahmana and Kshatriya rulers of Sindh against Arab invaders. Jats and Khokhars joined the Hindu Shahiya Rajas of Punjab against Mahmud of Ghazni. Throughout the medieval period, the lower castes fought shoulder to shoulder with the upper castes and against the foreign invaders and tyrannical rulers.

The 'exploitation' by the upper classes noticeable today is because of the rigidity developed by the Hindus caste system after the Hindus got bereft of political power for a long time and a moral degeneration set in. There is sufficient evidence to show that on the eve of Islamic invasions, the Hindu social system did not suffer from the defects which it developed at a later stage. In the mean time the upper castes came to the rescue of the lower castes in distress and the lower castes fought under the banner of the upper caste Kshatriyas in the defence of freedom. So well coalesced was the Hindu social structure that it not only saved India from the fate of countries like Iran, Iraq, Syria and Egypt when they confronted the Islamic onslaught, but did not rest content till it had supplanted the Muslim political power in the land even though it took a thousand years to do so. Hindus had suffered only a military defeat against Muslim invaders. It was not a collapse of the Hindu social system.

Backward classes and forest dwellers went on growing under Muslim pressure. Their numbers and nomenclatures have proliferated. Muslim rule spread all over the country. Resistance to it by Hindus also remained widespread. Jungles abounded throughout the vast land and flight into them was the safest safeguard. That is why SC/ST people are found in every state in large numbers. During the medieval period, in the years and centuries of oppression, they lived almost like wild beasts in improvised huts in forest-villages, segregated and isolated, suffering and struggling. But by settling in the forests, these freedom fighters of medieval India were enabled to preserve their religion and their culture.

The forest-village dwellers, whether escapees or resisters, suffered untold privations. In their segregated clusters, they developed their own social norms, their own rules of behaviour, their own rigid codes of conduct. This sometimes resulted in tension between one low caste and another. This tyranny of one low caste over another is still prevalent rather than the oppression of Brahmanas over the lower castes.

This book attempts to portray the rise and recapitulate the role of some of these backward classes and tribes in the history of medieval India, the process of their proliferation and the contribution they made in the preservation of Hindu culture under Muslim rule. It is necessary to bear in mind that there are no such categories as scheduled castes, scheduled tribes, other backward castes, Harijans, Dalits and so on in the records of the medieval times. Such people are mentioned as Kahars, Telis, Ahirs, Mochis etc. by name. We shall also do the same. But we cannot avoid modern nomenclatures like Dalits, Harijans, backward castes, low castes, bonded labourers, etc. In this book the most commonly used word for them would be backward or low castes because there are no familiar names for many classes, clusters or groups of Scheduled Castes and Tribes although their number runs into hundreds.

Medieval people loved their homes, their villages, and their fields. What often forced them to flee into the jungles was the Muslim army, its principles of war and its terror tactics. Therefore, at the end a survey of the Muslim army vis-a-vis the backward classes has been given. Muslim rule had spread all over India by the fifteenth century. So the study of the Muslim army is carried only up to that century.

This is the main thesis of the present study. However, in the context one points needs to be clarified. The march of the armed creed of Islam subverted many ancient civilizations before it knocked at the gates of India. Here they came across the existence of the caste system and they took the short cut of clamping all blame of the defeat of Hindus on their caste system. They popularised a theory that Hindus in medieval India were defeated by Muslim invaders because the Hindu social system was dominated by the Brahmanical caste system in which the lower castes were oppressed and exploited by the upper castes. On the other hand, they say, Islam came to India with a message of social equality and human brotherhood. The following pages amply bear out that these assumptions are incorrect.

Muslim chronicles themselves prove without a shadow of doubt that it was the Hindu social system based on caste which not only withstood the Islamic onslaught but also defeated it in the long run, after the Hindu states had gone down one after another in various parts of the country. So far as the message of social equality and human brotherhood of Islam is concerned, it was confined to Muslims alone. Muslim chronicles themselves describe how even basic human rights were denied to non-Muslims, high or low. Muslim invaders did not come as friends of the Dalits. Muslim rulers did not treat the low castes any better than they treated the high castes. Hindus suffered repeated defeats on the battlefield because due to a weak state system, their armies were ill-organised and ill-equipped as compared to the

Muslim state system which was highly militarized and geared to total war. Hindus would have been wiped out if their social system had been as weak as their state system.

As we put the record straight, we find that the small and scattered class of trained and traditional Hindu warriors, mostly Rajputs, stood exhausted by the time of the Mughal invasion, having fought the earlier invaders at every step for well-nigh eight centuries — from the middle of the seventh to the end of the fifteenth. The leadership of Hindu resistance to Muslim rule thereafter was provided by what are termed the Backward Castes and the Dalits in present-day India. These classes had fought earlier under the leadership of Rajput Rajas and Zamindars. Now onwards they took up the leadership on themselves, and battled with the Mughal regime till the latter stood shattered by the middle of the eighteenth century. It is a different story that in the process the Backward Castes and the Dalits suffered grievously and found themselves in a bad shape by the time the Islamic nightmare was over. That story has yet to be put together from indigenous annals which historians have neglected so far. This study is only a beginning, based for the most part on medieval Muslim chronicles.

September, 1995 K.S. Lal

Abbreviations

Abdullah	:	*Tarikh-i-Daudi*
Afif	:	*Tarikh-i-Firoz Shahi* by Shama Siraj Afif
Ain	:	*Ain-i-Akbari* by Abul Fazl, trans. by H. Blochmann
A.N.	:	*Akbar Nama* by Abul Fazl, trans. by H. Beveridge
Babur Nama	:	*Memoirs of Babur,* trans. by Ms. A. Beveridge
Badaoni	:	*Muntakhab-ut-Tawarikh* by Abdul Qadir Badaoni, trans. by S.A. Ranking
Barani	:	*Tarikh-i-Firoz Shahi* by Ziyauddin Barani
Bernier	:	*Travels in the Moghul Empire* by Francois Bernier
C.H.I.	:	*Cambridge History of India*
E.D.	:	*History of India as told by its own Historians* by Henry Elliot and John Dowson.
Dorn	:	*History of the Afghans,* being the English trs. of Niamatullah's *Makhzan-i-Afghana*
Farishtah	:	*Gulshan-i-Ibrahimi* or *Tarikh-i-Farishtah* by Muhammad Qasim Hindu Shah Farishtah
Foster	:	*Early Travels in India,* edited by William Foster
Hodivala	:	*Studies in Indo-Muslim History*
Ibn Battuta	:	*Rehla of Ibn Battuta,* trans. by Mahdi Husain
Imp. Gaz.	:	*Imperial Gazetteers, Provincial Series*
Khafi Khan	:	*Mutakhab-ul-Lubab* by Khafi Khan

Manucci	:	*Storia do Mogor* by Niccolao Manucci
Minhaj	:	*Tabqat-i-Nasiri* by Minhaj Siraj
Niamatullah,	:	*Makhzan-i-Afghana* by Niamatullah
Nizamuddin	:	*Tabqat-i-Akbari* by Nizamuddin Ahmad
Pelsaert	:	*Jahangir's India* by Francisco Pelsaert
Rizqullah	:	*Waqiat-i-Mushtaqi*
P.I.H.C.	:	*Proceedings of the Indian History Congress*
J.A.S.B.	:	*Journal of the (Royal) Asiatic Society of Bengal*
J.R.A.S.	:	*Journal of the Royal Asiatic Society of Great Britain*
Yadgar	:	*Tarikh-i-Salatin-i-Afghana* by Ahmad Yagdar
Yahiya	:	*Tarikhi-i-Mubarak Shahi* by Yahiya Sarhindi.

Contents

I
Introduction

Problem Specified

Of late the attention of social and political concerns in India has been focussing on the Scheduled Castes (SCs), Scheduled Tribes (STs) and Other Backward Castes (OBCs). With other associated problems, there is awareness of the immensity of their numbers. Scheduled Tribes and Castes alone form about 25 per cent of the population of the country. "According to 1991 Census, the populations of the scheduled castes and scheduled tribes were 13.82 crores and 6.78 crores constituting 16.48 and 8.08 per cent respectively of the country's total population of 84.63 crores. As compared to 1981 Census (SC population 15.75 per cent and ST population 7.85 per cent of the total population) there has been slight increase in SC as well as ST population in the terms of percentage."[1] Besides, every state of the Indian Union is identifying its Other Backward Castes. Hence their numbers will also go up when compilation of their lists is completed.

The eleventh century Muslim savant, Alberuni, who came to India in the train of Mahmud of Ghazni speaks of the four traditional castes and eight sections of Antyajas (untouchable?) or workers in low professions such as fuller, shoemaker, juggler, fisherman, hunter of wild animals and birds. "They are occupied with dirty work, like the cleaning of the village and other services."[2] In his time their number in Hindustan was obviously not large. But their numbers and nomenclatures increased with the passage of time.

There were tribes inhabiting rather isolated and wild areas from early times with their own names and specialities. To these were added hordes or groups invading or entering India in the

---

1 *India 1993*, Publications Division, Government of India, January 1994, p. 223; also pp. 15-16.

2 Alberuni, I, pp. 100-102.

ancient period, that is, before the advent of Islam. Some of these are very well known such as the Greeks, the Parthians, the Sakas or Scythians, the Kushanas, the Hunas, etc. They were assimilated into the social and cultural mainstream of Hinduism. Some of them merged into the existing castes, others got new caste names, and still others joined tribal groups or clusters. But it was during the medieval period under Muslim rule — 712 to 1707 CE — that many castes and sub-castes of SCs, STs and OBCs came into being, to become more than 2,330 enumerated today. For sure, tribal population increased rapidly under Muslim rule to become the 70-million strong tribal community of India today. It is the largest population of this kind in the world.

The year 1993 was named the international year of the indigenous peoples. It is not as innocent as it looks. In many parts of the world the white nations systematically liquidated the original 'native' inhabitants of their countries. Since very few of them have now remained they are being preserved as "dangerous species" with the respectable appellation of "indigenous people" given to them. In the old world, Hindus too were called natives by the whites. Now they are not termed so, but, in accordance with the old divisive policy, the words "indigenous Indians" are used for tribal and backward classes. The fact is that upper class Indians are as much indigenous as the lower, and the word need not be used in the Indian context. But since the word has become current in modern English usage, we too have to use it for tribal and backward classes primarily, however fallacious it may be. (And since the year 1993 was named after them the indigenous people of India also celebrated it by holding tribal youth cultural camps. A 15-day camp was held on the outskirts of Delhi at Holambi Khurd village where participants from Gujarat, Rajasthan, Mizoram, Nagaland, Orissa, Madhya Pradesh, Himachal Pradesh and Karnataka established contact through the medium understood by all — dance and music.) It is proposed here to trace their growth in historical perspective. It is also proposed to study the role of these sections of society in the political, cultural and religious spheres in the history of medieval India.

Source Materials

A precise study of the growth and activities of SCs, STs and OBCs under Muslim rule is difficult to make because our source materials are hopelessly deficient in information in this area. Our main authorities are the medieval chronicles. These have been written by Muslim ulema mainly in the Persian language, although there are a few treatises in Arabic and Turki also. Some Muslim chroniclers were prolific writers. For example, Mir Khwand's *Rauzat-us-Safa*, Farishtah's *Gulshan-i-Ibrahimi* and Abul Fazl's *Akbar Nama* run into thousands of pages. But prolific or concise, they confine their writings to narrating the "glorious victories of the faithful" or the conversion of the "infidels to the true faith". They do not care to study the indigenous Hindu society at all, not to speak of its complexities and ramifications. Some tribals and backward classes also have preserved their legendary accounts, their oral mystic traditions and their sacred groves and burial grounds, but only some. These two sources — the Muslim chronicles eulogizing their conquerors and kings no end, and the traditional accounts of tribals singing the praise of their victories over attackers and oppressors — help in reconstructing an interesting, though somewhat disjointed, account of Scheduled Castes and Scheduled Tribes in the medieval period.

To these sources of information may be added the Census reports of early British rule (chronologically closer to the medieval times) as well as the Gazetteers prepared in late nineteenth century and published in 1908-09. These have proved useful in listing the nomenclatures and vocations of most of the medieval tribes and castes. Consequently, the Gazetteers have been extensively used and referred to in the body of the book, instead of other contemporaneous accounts which the compilers of the Gazetteers must have taken care of in any case. Moreover, since we are covering the whole of the medieval period, it is more profitable to look to the Gazetteers for the activities of the low castes and tribes rather than to other medieval literature which is couched in pompous and turgid language containing minimum information

In this connection, however, it would be well to remember that in medieval times there were no categories or epithets as formulated in the Gazetteers like Animists, Aboriginals, Adivasis, Vanvasis, Vanputras, Nomads, Backwards, Tribals, Original or Indigenous inhabitants etc., etc. This categorization is modern; rather it is a formulation of the British compilers of the Gazetteers. Thus the Gazetteers are not without their politics. The British officials labelled the tribals, in successive Censuses, as Aboriginals (1881), Animists (1891-1911), and as Adherents of Tribal Religions (1921-1931). This is one example of how colonial notions of tribes and castes were imposed upon some sections of our population, although the communities concerned had gone through varied processes of transformation. It must be admitted that the terms 'caste' and 'tribe' can be only loosely used. "It has been aptly said that 'caste' is the largest group based on common occupation, and 'tribe' the largest group based on common descent."[3] But in actual usage they get mixed up. Mahatma Gandhi called the lowest castes Harijans, Dr. Ambedkar called them Depressed Castes, a term later translated as Dalit, while the Constitution classifies them as Scheduled Castes and Scheduled Tribes. Many other sections call themselves Other Backward Castes.[4]

These names have been given by modern anthropologists, sociologists, and political leaders. Naturally, medieval chroniclers do not mention them by these names. Instead they mention some tribes by their names like Jats, Bhils, Gonds, Kunbis, and some castes by their occupational denominations like Chamars, Lohars and Kahars. The one lower caste they repeatedly mention is Kahar.[5] Furthermore, they mention about people turning from

3 *Imp. Gaz.*, Bombay Presidency, I, p. 43.

4 They are still being classified and categorised, State-wise, for fixing their reservation quotas.

5 E.g., Barani, pp. 86 ff.; Afif, pp. 83, 325, 329; *Ain*, I, p. 264.

civilized life in urban and rural habitats to 'savage' existence in the forests. But it is possible to read between the lines and see the economic exploitation of the people which drove them to run away from settled life. In the medieval period under Muslim rule many Rajas, Zamindars and peasants were reduced from high class position to the status of scheduled caste and scheduled tribe forest dwellers. There were two ways in which high class people drifted into lower classes. One way was war, which was of perennial occurrence under Muslim rule. Generally speaking, cultivators who stayed on as Hindus on their land after defeat drifted into scheduled or other backward castes, whether they were enslaved or just made to work for the conquerors on sundry duties. Those who did not surrender and took to flight and established themselves in inaccessible jungles or mountain recesses became scheduled tribes, etc., generally speaking. The other way was the years and centuries of oppressive tax collection processes which compelled people to abandon their lands and seek shelter in the wilds. For, the majority of the then population was engaged in or associated with agriculture or its auxiliary cottage industries. The great number of SCs, STs and OBCs found today indicates that all sections of Hindu society in medieval times contributed in the process so as to swell their ranks so frightfully in our own times. Those who fought in the wars and fled were comparatively few. The largest number was of the oppressed peasants, artisans and labourers who drifted from the good and peaceful agrarian life towards low caste or tribal status. With long and permanent stay in forests or in hiding, many of these communities got new nomenclatures and their numbers multiplied.

Range of Muslim Rule

Since we shall be tracing the growth and narrating the activities of the Hindu lower classes in medieval India, it would be pertinent to give here the main benchmarks of Muslim rule for the benefit of the general reader who may not be quite familiar with its history. Muhammad bin Qasim invaded Sindh in 712 CE and Mahmud of Ghazni mounted seventeen campaigns in

Punjab, Sindh, Gujarat and Uttar Pradesh from 1000 to 1027. The victory of Muhammad Ghauri over Prithviraj Chauhan in 1192 heralded the establishment of regular Muslim rule in northern India. Muslim rule obtained in most parts of the country with varying degrees of effectiveness from the thirteenth to the eighteenth century. The rule of the Turks comprised three dynasties — the Slave (1206-1290), the Khalji (1290-1320) and the Tughlaq (1320-1414). Timur's invasion (1399-1400) rang the death knell of the centralized Sultanate of the Turks. The country broke up into small sultanates of Gujarat, Malwa, Deccan, Jaunpur, Bengal etc. in which Muslim rule and Muslim law continued to prevail. In Delhi, the Turks were followed by the Saiyyads (1414-1451), the Lodis (1451-1526), and the Surs (1540-1556). They completed the pre-Mughal Muslim rule in India called the Sultanate period. The Mughals ruled from 1526 to 1707 effectively, and from 1707 to 1857 with power declined. This brief resume has been given to help the reader assess the contribution of Muslim invaders and rulers to the growth and proliferation of the 'low caste' people under Muslim rule.

II
Tribes and Castes all Staunch Hindus

What are separately classified as Scheduled Castes, Schedules Tribes and Other Backward Castes in modern times were, in the medieval period, known and treated as one entity — the Hindu society. During that period of time all high and low castes were counted as Hindu and when Muslim invasions began all of them fought against Muslim invaders and rulers. All so-called low castes fought against Muslim invaders and rulers with as great determination and zeal as any high caste Rajas or Zamindars. In medieval times, Hindu castes and tribes were spread all over India. A brief resume of these classes would help appreciate the important role they played in the political, social, religious and economic history of medieval India.

Eastern India

Let us begin with Eastern India, comprising mainly Eastern Bengal, Assam and Northeastern States. The early inhabitants of Eastern Bengal and Assam comprised of Garos, Rabhas, Mechs, Mikris, Lalungos, Lushais, Kukis, Koches, Manipuris, Nagas, Khasis, Miris, Ahoms and many others. Before some of them became Muslims and Christians, they were all reckoned as Hindus. For example, Ahoms (a Shan tribe) willingly converted to Hinduism from 'Animism' (an artificial differentiation from Hinduism created by British anthropologists and administrators). These tribes worship a whole pantheon of Hindu gods and goddesses.[1] They celebrate Holi, Rath Yatra, Janmashtami, Kali and Durga Pujas and Baisakh Bihu or the advent of the Hindu new year. In Goalpara, the term Koch has been abandoned for the more honourable Hindu word 'Rajbansi' or 'men of the royal race'. Koch and Bodo tribes are synonymous. All places where

1 *Imp. Gaz.*, Eastern Bengal and Assam, pp. 34, 49-50, 214, 239.

Pods are found are studded with old Hindu temples. The (old British) Rajshahi Division must originally have formed part of the old kingdom of Paundra or Pundra-vardhana, the country of the Pods.[2] In Chittagong Hill Tracts the Chakmas and Maghs are Buddhists while Tipperas are Hindus. Manipuris are mostly Hindu and claim to be Kshatriya or Brahmana.[3]

In medieval Bengal, which included Bihar and Orissa also, a similar situation obtained. Bhumij, Kol (or Munda), Ho and Oraon tribes all called themselves Hindu.[4] In the 24 Paraganas, the Pods are the most numerous. They were divided into two classes, Padma Raj or Vratya Kshatriya, living by cultivation and regarding themselves as superior to the fishing Pods, but all considering themselves as Hindus.[5] In Gaya district, the aboriginal tribes of Bhuiyas, Dosadhs, Musahars and Rajwars were counted as 'semi-Hinduized' tribes.[6] (What is meant by, 'semi-Hinduised' has not been explained by the British compilers of the Gazetteers.) In the Santhal Parganas of Bhagalpur Division, the Santhals of aboriginal stock like Bhumijs, Hos and Mundas were returned in decennial Censuses as Hindus (and 'Animists'). According to the 1901 Census, they numbered 6,63,000.[7] In Orissa, all aboriginal tribes, both of Dravidian and Mongoloid origins, consider themselves as Hindu. They as well as Kurukh or Oraon have even abandoned their tribal language in favour of a local form of Hindi.[8] In spite of this, as Anwar Shaikh points out, Europeans' "low opinion of India prompted them to call aborigines of various countries as 'Indians'."[9]

It is not known as to when Bodo, Mech, Koch, Kachari, Rabha, Garo and Tippera tribes came to Assam and East Bengal but they are found spread all over North and East Bengal. The

2 *Imp. Gaz.*, Bengal, I, pp. 249-51.
3 Ibid., I, p. 360.
4 *Imp. Gaz.*, Eastern Bengal and Assam, pp. 51, 59, 200.
5 Ibid., pp. 372 ff., 410, 516, 618.
6 *Imp. Gaz.*, Bengal, II, pp. 35, 149.
7 Ibid., II, p. 223.
8 Ibid., II, pp. 250-412, esp. pp. 350-51.
9 Anwar Shaikh in *Liberty*, Humanist Quarterly, II, January 1995, pp. 39-40.

social structure of Bengal too was not coalesced. It was an amalgamation of Hindus, 'non-Hindus', and foreigners. The invaders and immigrants from the side of Assam, Tibet and Burma were not confirmed Hindus. In Assam and Bengal and also in Bihar and Orissa, the proportion of orthodox Hindus was small. No wonder, there caste as a fourfold classification ceases.[10] Besides, in the early period, there was rivalry between Buddhist and Hindu rulers and so also between Buddhism and Hinduism.[11] The Pala rulers of Bengal were Buddhists, the Senas were Hindus. In spite of the damage caused by Bakhtiyar Khalji, both the creeds flourished side by side. Muslim pressure of proselytization was met by the Tantric practice of Shaktism and the revival of Hindu Bhakti by Sankaradeva and Chaitanya. The tribals of these areas universally revere the latter as Prabhu. Still, the defences of Chandals, Pods and some other tribes and classes sometimes crumbled before the ruthless onslaughts of Islam because Muslims freely used force to convert people to their faith. Later on, Christian missions also converted many tribals to Christianity. But the tribals of the Eastern region who accepted Islam or Christianity could not entirely forsake Hinduism. The freedom loving people retained, as permitted by the Hindu spirit of social and religious diversity, their local beliefs, forms of devotion, folk tales and folk cultures with their own music and dance forms. They also preserved their original dialects and languages. All this has rendered Hinduism as their first love.

Central India

As per the *Imperial Gazetteer of India,* published in 1909, "the country now comprised in the Central Agency was probably once occupied by the ancestors of Bhils, Gonds, Saharias, and other tribes which now inhabit the fastnesses of the Vindhya

---

10 Ahmad Hasan Dani, 'Race and Culture Complexion in Bengal' in *Social Research in East Pakistan*, ed. P. Bessaignet, Asiatic Society of Pakistan, Dacca, 1960, pp. 93-110.

11 R.C. Mitra, *The Decline of Buddhism in India,* Vishvabharati, 1954, pp. 78-79.

range,"[12] while British Bundelkhand extends to the jungles of Central India. During the fifth and sixth centuries a number of nomad tribes — the Gurjaras, the Malavas, the Abhiras and many others who were probably descended from Central Asian invaders at the beginning of the Christian era — began to form regularly constituted Hindu communities. There is no historical record to show that these people were not Hindus. They had become part and parcel of Hindu civilization through the gradual process of assimilation in keeping with its spirit of inclusiveness. Kalachuris (Haihaya or Chedi) joined the Rajput clans and adopted the Hindu pantheon, as did the Paramaras of Dhar, Tonwars of Gwalior, Kachhwahas of Narwar, Rathors of Kanauj, and Chandelas of Kalinjar. The Gurjaras were in power in Central India in the eighth century — Gujarat is called so after them.[13]

Gondwana in Central India is the home of Gonds, a 'Dravidian' tribe bearing that name. The name Gondwana was given to it by Muhammadan historians. To its east lies Jharkhand or Chota Nagpur, to its west Malwa, to its north Panna. A large area of Gondwana was and is covered by jungles. The 1901 Census enumerated its population as two and a half million.

In the medieval period, the Gonds enjoyed a high degree of civilization and prosperity. The Gond ruling dynasty held most of (the old) Central Provinces from the fourteenth to the eighteenth century. "Even the far-reaching power of Akbar and the fanatic zeal of Aurangzeb made themselves but faintly felt at so great a distance from the seat of empire."[14] The tribe has two main divisions — the Raj Gonds who form the aristocracy and Dhur (or Dust) Gonds who comprise the commoners. They are a cultivating class and Brahmanas accept water from them; some scholars even suggest that Gonds are descended from Gaur Brahmanas. Today they are found all over the country — from Baghelkhand in the North to Hyderabad in the South as

12 *Imp. Gaz.*, Central India, p. 15.

13 Ibid., p. 18.

14 *The Gazetteer of the Central Provinces of India*, ed. Sir Charles Grant, p. xlviii. Also *Imp. Gaz.*, Bombay Presidency, I, pp. 115-121.

spillovers from the main block. The heart of Gondwana is still occupied in force by the Gonds. The plains of Chhattisgarh up to Godavari form another Gond stronghold. There are Gonds in Betul, Chhindwara, Seoni and Mandla. There are Kurkus in Hoshangabad, and Bhils in Nimar. There are also Baigas, Dhangars and Gadbas (in Bastar especially). But the Gonds outnumber all.[15] The Ethnological Committee compute that there are twenty-three certain and six doubtful aboriginal races in the Central Provinces.[16]

The Gonds have played a respectable role in the history of medieval India. As we shall see later on, they have witnessed great political vicissitudes of fortune, and have survived. They still enjoy a high degree of culture. Their religion is Hindu. Some even retain the sacred thread. Some of their Gods like Thakur Deo, Dulha Deo and Burha Deo command respect among local Hindus. The most interesting thing about their marriage customs is that they are similar to those prevalent among Koch and Bodo tribes of the Northeast.[17]

Migration of peoples, customs and ideas was as much prevalent in medieval India as it is in modern times. But with a difference. In modern times people generally move out because of choice; in medieval times they migrated because of compulsion. People in the medieval period loved their place of birth and domicile. They liked to live in their own villages under the joint family protection. But once their homes were threatened, they had no hesitation in moving away, even to far off places. The vastness of the country had inculcated in them the habit of traversing long distances. So Gonds and Bhils, ever fighting and struggling, are found as far south as Hyderabad in the Deccan.[18]

Since we have mentioned south, we may briefly mention some of the tribes of the South although they do not play as important a part in the history of India as the Jats, the Khokhars,

---

15 *The Gazetteer of the Central Provinces of India,* 273-278.
16 Ibid., p. cxx.
17 Ibid.
18 *Imp. Gaz.*, Hyderabad State, p. 24.

the Barwars, the Gonds and the Bhils of North India. The Yadava dynasty of Devagiri went down after ruling for about one hundred and thirty years when Harpal Deva was killed by the Khalji armies in 1318 CE. After this the Yadavas declined in status as well as importance both in the South and the North. The low castes in the Deccan comprised Malas, Dhers and Madigas of Telingana corresponding to the Mahars and the Mangs of the Maratha tract. Gottas or Dhangars (shepherds), Salas (weavers), Gaundlas (toddy drawers and liquor vendors), Lamanis or Banjaras (grain carriers) were some other tribes. Chamars were in large numbers in the South as in the North.[19] According to the 1901 Census there were four hundred and fifty communities in Madras Presidency from Brahmanas to the lowest caste. Some of the low castes were Kapus, Pallis, Vallalas, Paraiyars and Malas.[20] Vallalas was an Oriya caste. Mavikars were there in Malabar as were also Moplahs (Muslim) and Nayars (Hindu). In marked contrast to Gujarat with its amplitude of caste divisions, the Deccan contains a comparatively homogeneous population.

Many of these tribes in Eastern and more so in Central India were highly civilized in their own way. For example, there is no infanticide among Gonds and Santhals. Among the Santhals, girls are married as adults mostly to men of their own choice. Sexual relation before marriage is tacitly recognized. The young man is bound to marry a girl if she becomes pregnant. If attempts are made to evade the obligation, he is severely beaten by the *jog-manjhi* (or chief), and, in addition to this, his father is required to pay a heavy fine.[21] Similarly, among the Oraons unmarried males sleep in a bachelor's dormitory (*dhumkuria*) and marriage does not take place until after the girls have attained the age of puberty.[22] "The Maria Gonds consider the consent of the girl to be an essential preliminary. She gives it before a council of

19 Ibid., p. 144, also pp. 23-24.
20 *Imp. Gaz.*, Madras, I, pp. 30-31.
21 *Imp. Gaz.*, Bengal, II, p. 224.
22 Ibid., I, p. 251.

elders, and if necessary is allowed time to make up her mind."[23]

It is not only in the social and religious domain that there was a sense of social cohesion. In the economic sphere also there was development together with inter-change in vocations. In the eastern Vindhyan region there was great tribal contiguity of hunters, cattle-growers, artisans, mendicants, itinerant traders and others, for example in Bastar district. The flourishing craft of iron-smelting and forging among Agarias before the "on-slaught of modern forest laws" has sucked the life out of this craft. Colonel Ward, Settlement Officer of Mandla district (1869), dismissed the great Agaria tradition in these words: "Agarias are inefficient and lazy." His mistaken reason was that Agarias invariably located their furnaces close to the sources of ore. "Tribal social cohesion could never have survived were it not for the fact that pre-modern political economy allowed for the co-existence of diverse modes of livelihood."[24] The Pahadia tribals in the Santhal Parganas have a similar history of colonial prejudice.

Western India

In the west of Central India, that is, in Malwa, Gujarat, Maharashtra and Rajasthan, there were a large number of backward tribes and castes with their independent primitive societies, besides of course pure-blooded Rajput clans. In Rajputana Bhils were the most numerous in south and south-west. Of all the lower castes like Jats, Gujars, Balais (village servants), Malis, Kachhis, Gadris, Dhakars, Telis and Kumhars, the Bhils were the largest in number in Udaipur, Banswara and Dungarpur.[25] Bhilwara city in Rajasthan derives its name from them. They were actually found everywhere except the eastern states. In 1901 they numbered about three and a half lakhs of whom about sixty-six per cent were in Mewar and Banswara. Jats were numerous in some other states like Jaipur (10 per cent), Jodhpur (11 per

---

23 *Imp. Gaz.*, Central India, p. 119.

24 Suresh Sharma, *Tribal Identity and the Modern World,* Sage Publishers, New Delhi, 1994.

25 *Imp. Gaz.*, Rajputana, pp. 68-90, 117, 148, 161-68, 221.

cent), Bikaner (22 per cent), and Kishangarh.[26] A section of the Jats called Bishnois are vegetarians and teetotallers.[27] The Bishnois have earned world-wide appreciation for their love of trees. Once a Raja of Jodhpur wanted some timber for construction in his palace. The Bishnois clasped the trees, remained clung to them and got themselves cut down rather them suffer the trees to be destroyed. Another Jat caste is of Sinsinwars and a third one of Churaman and Khem Karan Jats. As we shall see later, in Uttar Pradesh and in many places in Rajasthan the Chamars, also called Balais, were more numerous than Jats and Bhils.

Of the wild or semi-civilized tribes, mention may be made of Kolis, Berads, Varlis, Thakurs, Vanjaras and Ahirs. Among shepherds and herdsmen may be included Dhangars, Kurabas and Bharvads. The low caste and menials included Dhers, Mahars and Holias, Mochis and Chamars, and Mangs. The artisans comprehended Lohars, Sutars (carpenters), Sonars, Darzis, Kumhars, Bhandaris, Malis (farmers), Hajjams and Nhavis.[28] In the erstwhile Bombay Presidency there were about five hundred main endogamous castes or tribes who married within their group. Some of the important ones, excluding those already mentioned above, are Kunbis (other than Maratha Kunbis), Kolis or Koris (chiefly weavers and labourers), Lingayats (Shaivite Hindus), Telis and Chanchis and Rabaris.[29] In Sindh, because of Islamic influence, Muslim tribes have a leading place, while castes are relegated to a subordinate position. The castes of Sindh are Bhil, Dher or Mahar, Khitri, Koli, Kurmi, Mazhala, Sikh, Muslim Jat and Muhanas (fishermen), Shikari, Sonar, Vani (trader of low caste), etc.[30] In Cutch and Kathiawar, there are Ahirs (shepherds who entered at an early date), Bhils and Kolis, Dhodhias and Dhankas and curiously enough Chamars as artisans.[31]

26 Ibid., pp. 170-207, 241, 273, 406.
27 Ibid., p. 180.
28 *Imp. Gaz.*, Bombay Presidency, I, p. 45.
29 Ibid., pp. 43-44.
30 Ibid., I, p. 47; II, pp. 241-42, 303.
31 Ibid., II, pp. 354, 426, 452.

The Bhils who mainly reside in the hilly country between Abu and Asirgarh and have also spread into the plains of Gujarat and spilled over into northern Deccan, are Hindus. Some even claim to be reckoned as Rajputs. But many of their sub-tribes or *kuls* pay no respect to the Brahmanas or Hindu Gods, nor do they build temples. They worship only Devi, but celebrate Holi, Dushera and Diwali like other Hindus.[32] They have always remained Hindu. It is not only among the Bhils but all over the country that many tribes have as many forms of Hinduism as are permitted by the Hindu spirit of accommodating social and religious diversities.

Northern India

Turning from western to northern India, there were in Uttar Pradesh in the medieval period as of now, Chamars, Ahirs, Brahmanas, Rajputs, Koris, Kurmis and the Bhars. They have all lived, the high and the low, as part of the Hindu civilization. Curiously enough, the most numerous caste of Uttar Pradesh was, in about 1900 or at the end of the medieval period, the Chamars. As per the *Imperial Gazetteer*, "Musahars, Dosadhs and Chamars may be considered semi-Hinduized aborigines",[33] but this is unnecessary hairsplitting. All these castes were full-fledged Hindus, as vouched by Alberuni. Chamars formed the largest groups in the districts of Saharanpur, Muzaffarnagar, Meerut, Bulandshahr, Aligarh, Mathura and Agra,[34] as well as in Banda, Kalinjar, Jhansi, Jalaun, Hardoi, Kheri, Fyzabad and several other districts like Jaunpur, Azamgarh and Ghazipur.[35] In Meerut and Bulandshahr districts, Chamars were the most numerous, comprising 20 per cent of the population. So also was the case in Aligarh, Agra and Mathura.[36] In Banda and Jalaun too they formed the largest class. But let not the list be made too exhaustive.

32 *Imp. Gaz.*, Central India, pp. 81-85.

33 *Imp. Gaz.*, Bengal, II, p. 35, repeated on p. 168.

34 *Imp. Gaz.*, United Provinces of Agra and Oudh, I, pp. 273, 294, 310, 335, 356, 372, 395.

35 Ibid., II, pp. 36, 54, 90, 112, 232, 353, 366, 380.

36 Ibid., I, pp. 353, 372, 395; II, pp. 54, 112.

The point to emphasise is that Chamars formed a very important Hindu caste.[37] It was engaged in leather work and cultivation. Besides being carriers, tanners, day-labourers, village menials and agriculturists, they were also craftsmen withal. In conjunction with people of other castes, they fought against foreign invaders and oppressive rulers·

Here a word may be said about the two upper castes— Brahmanas and Kshatriyas — to compare them with Chamars. In U.P. Brahmanas were the most numerous caste in Allahabad and Varanasi districts as these were centres of Hindu pilgrimage.[38] In Varanasi, "Brahmans were a little more than Chamars".[39] Elsewhere Chamars were the most numerous. It was not only in U.P. but, as seen earlier, they were in large numbers all over India — in Rajasthan, in Cutch and Gujarat and even in the South. In U.P. as a whole, according to the 1931 Census, Brahmanas were the largest amongst the higher castes — 10.9 per cent — and Chamars the largest amongst the lower castes — 15.1 per cent.[40] The upper castes might have sometimes submitted to force or

---

37 In Bhandar (near Raipur in M.P.), the headquarters of the Satnami Chamars, "every fourth man is a Chamar", and nearly all are cultivators (Grant, *Central Provinces*, p. 100).

38 *Imp. Gaz.*, United Provinces of Agra and Oudh, II, p. 67.

39 Ibid., II, p. 123.

40 Based on the U.P. Census Report of 1931:

Table

Showing some Hindu low Castes of U.P.

	Per cent of caste Members adhering to Hindu Religion	Per cent of each caste in Total Religious Membership
Chamar	99.7	15.1
Ahir	97.7	9.4
Kurmi	99.7	4.2
Pasi	100.0	3.5
Kahar	99.1	2.8
Lodh	99.7	2.6
Gadariya	99.6	2.4
Kori	99.9	2.2
Kumhar	98.7	1.9
Teli	74.8	1.8
Kachi	99.9	1.7

temptation, but not the Chamars. For example, in Muzaffarnagar district there were 29,000 Hindu Rajputs and 24,000 Muslim Rajputs according to the 1901 Census. Similarly, there were Hindu Rajputs and Muslim Rajputs in almost equal numbers in many western districts of U.P.[41] In eastern U.P. there were Muslim Pathans and converted Rajputs, as for instance 34,000 each in Basti district.[42] The reason for this phenomenon was that some Rajputs who loved their religion more than their land fought against Muslim invaders to the last. Many perished in the encounters. Those who survived, survived as Hindu Rajputs. Those who loved their land more than their religion converted to Islam to retain their lands and kingdoms. Let only one instance of this suffice. When Raja Har Dutt of Baran (Bulandshahr in western U.P.) was informed about Mahmud of Ghazni's invasion, "he feared for his life, which was forfeited under the law of God. So he reflected that his safety would best be secured by conforming to the religion of Islam, since God's sword was drawn from the scabbard. He came forth, therefore, with ten thousand men, who all proclaimed their anxiety for conversion ..." [43] Such cases were not rare throughout the medieval period. They debunk the theory that low caste people converted to Islam more easily than the high castes. The Chamars did not convert, as their large numbers show. Of course, there are no Muslim Chamars. A few, however, belong to the higher profession of shoe-makers.

The other low caste Hindus found in numbers in Uttar Pradesh are Minas and Meos of Mewat, though Hindu Jats are not found east of Rohilkhand. Others like Ahars or Ahirs and Khajis are excellent cultivators, resembling the Lodhas of the Doab.[44] Malis, Saini Tagis, Gujars (cultivators, graziers and land holders), Kahars, Bajgis (singers and musicians), Koris (aborigines, now weavers and labourers), Kurmis and Kachhis (cultivators, market-gardeners), Gadarias

---

41 *Imp. Gaz.*, United Provinces of Agra and Oudh, I, p. 294.
42 Ibid., II, p. 223.
43 *Tarikh-i-Yamini*, E. D., II, pp. 42-43.
44 *Imp. Gaz.*, United Provinces of Agra and Oudh, I, p. 248.

(shepherds), Telis and Julahas (both Hindu and Muslim), Bhangis (sweepers), Pasis (toddy drawers and labourers), Lunis (saltpetre workers) etc., are and were there in good numbers.

West of U.P., the Punjab of medieval India had a large number of high and low tribes, Hindu and Muslim. The pressure of Muslim invaders and immigrants from abroad was the heaviest in the Punjab throughout the medieval period. Therefore, most of the tribes were bifurcated into Hindu and Muslim and later on trifurcated into Hindu, Muslim and Sikh. Thus the Jats, found all over northern India, are almost equally divided into Hindu, Sikh and Muslim. Many Rajputs too became Muhammadans. "The Hindu Rajputs are found mainly in the north-east corner of the Province, and in the Himalayan and submontane tracts, the Rajput tribes of the plains having for the most part accepted Islam." [45]

In the Salt Range, north of the erstwhile Punjab province (comprising Haryana and Punjab of India and Pakistan), the Jats, the Awans, the Kakars, the Gakhars and the Khokhars were well entrenched. The Jats, Hindu as well as Sikh, fought Muslim invaders and rulers throughout. In the end they gathered sufficient strength to found their own kingdoms. The Gakhars claim to have come with Mahmud of Ghazni. Their chieftains were most loyal to the house of Babur. Sher Shah built the Rohtas fort in Jhelum district to overcome the Gakhars of the Salt Range, who had long been vassals or allies of the Mughals. They flourished and fell with the Mughals. They are still found in strength in Rawalpindi district.[46] Kakars are Afghans and inhabit northern Baluchistan. Zhob Kakars are the indigenous and principal tribe of Afganistan as are the Baloch, the Brahuis and the Lasis. Many Jats have been absorbed by the Baloch and the Brahuis.[47] The Khokhars are resident Indians. Their stronghold was the Salt Range. They fought against the foreigners relentlessly, first as

45 *Imp. Gaz.*, Punjab, I, p. 49.
46 Ibid., II, pp. 144, 161.
47 *Imp. Gaz.*, Baluchistan, pp. 27, 102, 103.

Hindus, and later as Muslims after conversion.[48]

In the Simla Hills, Kanet form the most important element, the Dogras and Kolis as the principal menial tribes. In Kangra, during the Muhammadan period, the Katoch princes were driven into the hills where their fortresses already existed. But many of them gradually turned into tribals.

The lower castes in the Punjab comprised the Chamars, Chuhras, Musallis and Dhanaks (scavengers), Jhinwars (water carriers), Kumhars (potters), Lohars (blacksmiths), Nais (barbers), Tarkhans (carpenters), Telis (oil workers), Malis and Sainis (market-gardening tribes), and Julahas (cotton-carders). Other menial castes are Mochis (shoemakers and leather workers), Sonars (goldsmiths), Chhimbas and Dhobis (washermen), Machhis (fishermen and water carriers), Meghs (weavers), Mirasis (village minstrels), Barwalas and Batwals (village watchmen). The one special caste belonging to Punjab is that of Fakirs, in some places found in large numbers. Furthermore, besides a large number of converted tribals, "there are in many villages one or two families of a menial tribe from which the village watchmen are drawn, who are said to be the relics of the old policy of the emperors of settling one or two Muhammadans in every village."[49] Bawaris, Harnis and Sansis have been proclaimed as criminal tribes.[50] Gurgaon district abounds in Meos. They are the same stock as Minas of the Aravalli Hills. They fought the Muslims for long. but eventually succumbed to become Muslim. Now, although almost all have become Muhammadan, they have retained Hindu customs which are now under attack of *tablighis.* Kashmiris are also found in many districts of the Punjab. Many Kashmiris had escaped into these districts around 1400 CE when Sikandar Butshikan of Kashmir, by the end of his reign, had converted probably all Hindu inhabitants of the Valley except the Brahmanas.[51]

48 For Gakhars, Kakars and Khokhars see *Ain.*, I, pp. 456, 486. Also Punjab Census Report, 1881, p. 149; *Indian Historical Quarterly*, XV, 1939, p. 49n; *Journal of the Asiatic Society of Bengal*, XL, 1871, Pt. I, p. 67; *Indian Antiquary*, XXXVI, pp. 1-8.

49 *Imp. Gaz.*, Punjab, I, p. 305.

50 Ibid., p. 443.

51 *Imp. Gaz.*, Kashmir and Jammu, p. 24.

We may close with a word on Nepal. According to the ancient chronicles kept in Nepal, the earliest dynasty was founded by eight Ahirs from Gujarat, followed by the same race from Hindustan. Adi Shankaracharya visited Nepal and reformed Hinduism. Gurkhas are originally from Rajasthan, whence they migrated early in the fourteenth century after the capture of Chittor by Alauddin Khalji.[52] The Khasas, the Magars, the Gurungs and the Thakurs are military tribes. "They are the descendants of the aboriginal tribes who intermarried with Rajputs and other Hindus who took refuge from Muhammadan conquest in the hills of Nepal in the twelfth century. ... These are Gurkhas and Gurkhalis." Newars, the original inhabitants, are the largest in numbers as are the Bhotias, Murmis and Limbus. "The Tharus and Boksas are distinct... and are more akin to the aboriginal tribes of India. They inhabit the Tarai and low-lying valleys which open into it."[53] Hinduism and Buddhism have been flourishing together. "In fact, Hindus and Buddhists may often be seen worshipping at the same shrine."[54]

Hinduism: India's Indigenous Religion

In the preceding pages only a few tribes and castes residing in India in the medieval period have found a mention. Their classification as living in eastern or western India is only pragmatic. There were large core clusters in some specific areas while spillover groups were found in many other parts also. For example, Bhils belonging largely to Rajasthan are found in Andhra Pradesh also, as are Chodhara and Davacha in Karnataka. So much so that "the Bhils have long ceased to be a homogeneous people. One can see a wide range of physical types and complexions" among them.[55] In the medieval period, as of now, Backward Castes, Scheduled Castes and Scheduled Tribes

52 *Imp. Gaz.*, Afghanistan and Nepal, p. 99, also pp. 96-97 for early history. Also see Appendix A, "Alauddin and Nepal", in Lal, *Khaljis*, pp. 347-49.

53 *Imp. Gaz.*, Afghanistan and Nepal, pp. 108-109.

54 Ibid., p. 111.

55 Koenraad Elst, *Indigenous Indians*, pp. 181-82.

were spread all over the country without any such tags being attached to their major or minor units. Medieval Muslim chroniclers, who are our main source of information for the history of the middle ages in India, nowhere distinguish between tribals, low caste and high caste Hindus. And rightly so, because they did not find any such difference among them. For the information of "Letter to the Editor" writers, not a single Muslim chronicle ever says that social distinctions prompted low caste Hindus to abjure their faith and adopt Islam voluntarily. Alberuni, Abul Fazl and emperor Jahangir are some of the medieval writers who refer to the Hindu caste system in some detail. Jahangir indeed writes about the fourfold Hindu caste system or the Varnashrama Dharma in an appreciative vein.[56]

Since Muslim writers do not differ in their observations about the Hindu society, only Alberuni may be quoted at some length to appraise the situation. "The Hindus call their castes *varnas* i.e. *colours* ... These castes are from the very beginning only four (Brahmana, Kshatriya, Vaisya and Sudra)... Much, however, as these classes differ from each other, they live together in the same towns and villages, mixed together in the same houses and lodgings ...." The Antyaja like shoemaker, hunter of wild animals etc. are divided into eight guilds. "The four castes do not live with them together in one and the same place. These guilds live near the villages and towns of the four castes, but outside them."[57] The tribals were (and are) not markedly different from surrounding populations. There was coexistence and mingling of cultures of various segments of the population. They have all lived together, fought a common enemy together, and shared joys and sorrows together. Their food is the same. Their forms of worship are similar, "... the endogamy and exogamy practices of the tribals and Sanskritic Hindus are essentially the same ..."[58]

56 *Tuzuk-i-Jahangiri,* I, pp. 244-47, 357-59.
57 Alberuni, I, pp. 100-101.
58 Koenraad Elst, op. cit., p. 201.

The principal tribes and castes in medieval India just did not become 'nominally' Hinduized to be continued strongly 'animistic' as stressed by some British writers.[59] These writers often laid great emphasis on differentiating Hindus from Animists and Aboriginals etc. But they had to concede that "no very strict line can be drawn between Animists and low-class Hindus".[60] They had also to admit that "the jungle tribes of Central India stoutly advance a claim to be considered Hindu".[61] Bhils, Gonds, Saharias have all the time belonged to Hinduism, the cardinal religion of India.[62]

In fact, as David Frawley notes, "Hinduism is often erroneously looked at as restricted to the subcontinent of India. However, historically Hinduism has been practised throughout much of the world, and teachings of the same order as Hinduism have flourished everywhere."[63]

"Hindus came from a number of different races and ethnic groups even within India. The people of Nepal, though a Mongolian race like the Tibetan and Chinese are predominantly Hindus in religion. Many tribal groups of India, many of which are not Caucasian or Mongolian but of the Austric race, are predominantly Hindu. Hinduism remains in Bali in Indonesia... Hinduism once dominated Indo-China wherein the Ankor Wat temple complex abound with Hindu temples. Vietnam was a Hindu

---

59 *Imp. Gaz.*, Central India, pp. 15, 113, 194.

60 *Imp. Gaz.*, Bombay Presidency, I, p. 47.

61 *Imp. Gaz.*, United Provinces of Agra and Oudh, I, p. 45.

62 Dr. B.R. Ambedkar writes about his choice of Buddhism thus: "I will choose only the least harmful way for the country and that is the greatest benefit I am conferring on the country by embracing Buddhism; for Buddhism is a part and parcel of *Bharatiya* culture. I have taken care that my conversion will not harm the tradition of the culture and history of this land" (Dr. Ambedkar, *Writings and Speeches*, Government of Maharashtra, III, p. 498).

Koenraad Elst adds that "one reason of his (Ambedkar's) embracing Buddhism was that he wanted a rational and humanist religion, for which the bizarre beliefs of Christianity and Islam did not qualify. Another reason was that it was an indigenous religion which would not bring with it extra-territorial loyalties" *(Indigenous Indians*, p. 391).

63 David Frawley, *Hinduism*, p. 78.

country up into the seventeenth century. Afghanistan was dominated by Hinduism into the tenth century. Hindu influence existed in Persia, Central Asia and Middle East, not only by Hindu traders but with Hindu converts. Even a number of ancient Greeks become Hindus".[64] Hinduism does not define the Hindu religion but simply identifies the region where it flourished.

"Hindus are not all of one faith. They are divided into Shaivites (those who worship Shiva), Vaishnavas (those who worship Vishnu), Shaktas (those who worship the Goddess) Ganapatyas (those who worship Ganesha) and a number of other groups which are constantly being revised. The tendency of Hinduism is not to coalesce into a fanatic unity but to disperse into various diverse sects and not to stick to any common deity or worship. Hinduism is a supertolerant religion. No other religion in the world accepts such a diversity of beliefs and practices and is so ready to acknowledge the validity of other religions."[65]

That being so, the Hindu tribals chose their own deities, their own Gods and Goddesses. They recognised God not only in human-like beings but even in animals and birds, in animate and inanimate objects. This fitted in within the larger perspective of Hindu tradition which did not believe in standardized, rigid and artificial system but a belief system or social system with freedom of spirit for creativity. Hindu culture has never suppressed domiciled cultures or been opposed to cultural variations. Hence the "religions" of the tribal people were acceptable to caste Hindus and vice versa. In this society, no one was rootless, no body belonged to an anonymous mass; everyone had a niche, a place where he was not a stranger; as a member of a great community, no one could be pushed around and he had the protection of the community. This society was free from coercive state apparatus.

One thing more. As Anwar Shaikh points out, "though worshippers were particularly enthusiastic about the greatness of the

---

64 Ibid., pp. 58-59.

65 David Frawley, *Arise Arjuna, Hinduism and the Modern World,* 1995, pp. 36, 37, 42, 43; *Hinduism,* pp. 119, 120-121.

statues they worshipped, they did not revile the idols of other devotees because of their belief that they too were divine for representing natural forces leading to the worship of all gods... In fact, the co-existence of idols prompted the attitude of 'live and let live.'"[66] That is how, as we shall see later on also, the Ahoms in the far eastern region willingly adhered to Hinduism and adopted a whole pantheon of Hindu Gods and Goddesses. All the tribes of Indo-Chinese origin in eastern India voluntarily "converted" to Hinduism, celebrating all Hindu festivals in Assam — Manipuris being the latest addition. This is the phraseology of the Gazetteers because all these people were Hindus from the very beginning; there was no question of their conversion to Hinduism — Hinduism is not a proselytizing religion. Similar is the case with the Gonds, the Bhils, the Korkus, the Kols, the Vokkaligas, the Kurubas, the Lingayats and hundreds of other communities. The professional groups of Chamars, Bhangis, Chandals etc. have remained almost exclusively Hindu. Curiously enough, under the ever mounting pressure of Islamic proselytization, many of these and many more turned still more staunch Hindus, adding rigidity to the caste system under Muslim rule.

66 Anwar Shaikh, 'Idolatory, Islam and India' in *Liberty*, January 1995, p. 18.

III
Conflict of Indian Tribes with Muslim Invaders

Jats and Meds oppose Muhammad bin Qasim

The first major Muhammadan invasion of Hindustan occurred in 712 CE when Muhammad bin Qasim Sakifi marched into Sindh. He was opposed by the rulers of Sindh militarily and politically. The history of this resistance is widely written about and well known today. What is not widely known is that Muhammad bin Qasim was also confronted by lower classes and tribal people like Jats and Meds, not only as serving soldiers of their rulers but also sometimes independently. The tribes that inhabited the region from Sindh to Baluchistan at this point of time were Tak, Kurk, Mina, Meds, Jats, Lohanas, Sammas and many others of lesser note or at least less easy to identify.[1] The Meds now, as then, lived on the coast. The Jats composed the cultivating classes. Some of the Kurks whose insolence led to the final subjugation of Sindh by the Arabs, are still found in Baluchistan.[2]

Muslim chroniclers affirm that Jats and Meds joined Muhammad bin Qasim when he invaded Sindh. They belonged to the lower rung of the prevailing Hindu social order and therefore they were hostile to the rulers because of the humiliation they had suffered under the discriminatory treatment of the Hindu government. This had embittered them and they flocked under the banner of the alien invader. The Sammas, another tribal people, welcomed Muhammad bin Qasim "with frolicks and merriment".[3]

This version of the Muslim chroniclers needs to be analysed in

---

1 Al Kufi, *Chachnama*, E.D., I, p. 187 and Elliot's Appendix, pp. 429-30.
2 *A Gazetteer of Baluchistan*, p. 27.
3 *Chachnama*, op. cit., I, p. 191.

depth. The king of Ceylon had sent to Hajjaj bin Yusuf Sakifi, the governor of the eastern provinces of the Caliphate, eight vessels filled with presents, Abyssinian slaves, pilgrims, and the orphan daughters of some Muslim merchants who had died in his dominions. The vessels were attacked and plundered by pirates off the coast of Sindh. Hajjaj sent a letter to Raja Dahir demanding reparations, but Dahir replied that the pirates were beyond his control and he was powerless to punish them. At this Hajjaj sent two expeditions (708 CE) against Debal, the first under Ubaidulla and the second under Budail. But both the expeditions failed; their commanders were killed and their armies routed.[4] Deeply affected by these failures, and on becoming convinced that any half-measures would not do, Hajjaj fitted out a third and impressive expedition and conferred the command of the campaign on his seventeen year old nephew and son-in-law Imaduddin Muhammad bin Qasim.

Now the pirates who had waylaid the ships and looted its treasures and women were the daring Meds.[5] They would not have served under the Arab invader. The Jats were faithful to their rulers; it is hard to believe that they were disloyal to the Hindu king. They sent fire-wood to the kitchen of the kings, and served them as menials and guards. "Whenever guides were required by the Kings," writes Al Kufi, they used to be engaged as professional escorts, and "the caravans used to travel day and night under their guidance." They used to take their dogs with them when they went out of doors, so that they may by this means be recognised (as guides?). If an injury befell a person on the road, these tribes had to answer for it. The best thing about them was that "there was no distinction among them of great and small".[6]

The narratives of Al Kufi and Al Biladuri are full of contradictions of praise and prejudice about the Jats and other tribes of Sindh

4 Farishtah, II, pp. 311-12.

5 Al Biladuri, *Futuh-ul-Buldan*, E.D., I, p. 118 and Elliot's Appendix, pp. 519-31; S.R. Chowdhry, *Al Hajjaj Ibn Yusuf*, p. 116.

6 *Chachnama*, E.D. I, p. 187.

like Lohana, Lakha and Samma. Muhammad bin Qasim was informed that they were not allowed to wear soft clothes, or cover their heads with velvet. They kept their heads and feet naked but used to throw a sheet of coarse cloth over their shoulders. Sisikar, the minister of (the later defeated) Raja Dahir, who had to join Muhammad bin Qasim, informed the latter that among them "no chief was permitted to ride on a horse", but contradicts himself in the next sentence when he says that "if any of their chiefs or Ranas rode upon a horse, he had no saddle or bridle, but threw a blanket on its back, and then mounted". This means that they had their leaders, "their chiefs or Ranas".[7] (Farishtah reminds us that rulers of small kingdoms are called Ranas in India.[8])

After praising them as being good guides to travellers and possessing a sense of equality among themselves, Al Kufi again reverts to denouncing them. "They have the disposition of savages... They plunder on the roads, and within the territory of Debal all join with them in their highway robberies."[9] Muhammad bin Qasim also declared: "What disgusting people (Jats and other tribes) are. They are just like the tribals of Persia and the mountains (*mardan-i-dashti* or people of jungles and wilds)." Qasim was an Arab; he was prejudiced against non-Arab Persians and Indians. But how can we reconcile all the contradictory statements of all others cited above? It would seem that some Jats and other tribals joined the invader during the initial Muslim intrusions, which had started as early as 636 CE. They appear to have become inimical to the Arabs after the latter destroyed the temple of Debal and other venerated shrines in Sindh, forcibly converted people to Islam, imposed the *jizyah* on the people, and sucked Sindh dry. Such was the extent of the loot of the Sindhis (120 million dirhams in cash alone),[10] that doles had to be given to merchants and artisans, agriculturists and Brahmins to rehabilitate

7 Ibid., I, pp. 151, 187.
8 Farishtah, I, p. 16
9 *Chachnama*, E.D., I, p. 187.
10 Al Biladuri, E.D., I., p. 123 and Elliot's Appendix, p. 470; S.R. Chowdhry, *Al Hajjaj*, p. 118.

themselves.[11] Worse still, as soon Muhammad bin Qasim had gained a foothold in the country, he treated the Jats and other tribes with scant consideration and "maintained the same (old humiliating) rules regarding them"— rules of discriminatory treatment attributed to high class Hindus.[12] Indeed, as Henry Elliot aptly points out, "the inhibition of riding on saddles and wearing fine clothes, baring the head, the accompaniment of a dog, the drawing of and hewing wood for the royal kitchen, were more suited to Musulman intolerance than the mild sway of Hinduism," and Muhammad Qasim imposed these "same conditions with even greater stringency than his predecessor."[13]

Furthermore, thousands of Jats were enslaved; some were made to serve in their native land, while others were sent out of the country. Muhammad bin Qasim sent 'Zutt', 'Sayabiya' and other tribals accompanied by their wives, children and herds of cattle to Al Hajjaj along with treasures during his campaign. Al Hajjaj forwarded part of the presents with large number of Zutts to Caliph Al Walid.[14] "From the seventh century onwards and with a peak during Muhammad al-Qasim's campaigns in 712-13," writes Andre Wink, "a considerable number of Jats was captured as prisoners of war and deported to Iraq and elsewhere as slaves."[15] The grandfather of Abu Hanifa, the great Sunni Imam and jurisconsult, was a native of Kabul and bore the name of Zuta.[16] 'Jats' here is obviously used as a generic term for all tribes, indeed for all Hindus. Many of them were enslaved by Muslim invaders and sent abroad. Many others fled the country to save themselves from enslavement and conversion. It is authentically believed that they form the bulk of the six million Gypsies found today all over Europe.[17] This sale of slaves, expulsion

11 *Chachnama*, E.D., I, pp. 160, 174-75, 182-185.
12 Ibid., p. 187.
13 Elliot's Appendix in E.D., I, p. 435.
14 Chowdhry, *Al Hajjaj*, p. 118 on the authority of Al Biladuri.
15 Andre Wink, *Al Hind*, p. 161.
16 T.P. Hughes, *Dictionary of Islam*, pp. 7-8.
17 D.P. Singhal, *India and World Civilization*, I, p. 234.

and exodus went on for many centuries. Their migration may have also formed the last trail of the Aryans who are now known to have slowly fanned out from India to various countries of Europe.[18]

After the sack of the temple of Debal in Sindh by Muhammad bin Qasim, the Jats had become staunch enemies of the Arab invaders and harassed them through guerrilla warfare in the form of highway robbery. In this act of vengeance the Jats were joined by other Sindhi victims. Masudi who visited India in 915-16 CE, about two hundred years after Qasim's invasion, states that the Meds were at constant war with the people of Mansura,[19] a Muslim colony established after Qasim's departure from Sindh. The Jats also once invaded the principality of Mansura and forced its Musalman Amir to abjure his religion.[20] There was no looking back for these tribesmen as regards their animosity to Muslim invaders and rulers in India. The Jats grew very powerful after the break-up of the Hindu Shahiya kingdom of Lahore by the Ghaznavids. They made devastating raids into the neighbouring districts. They molested Mahmud Ghaznavi's army on its return journey from Somnath.

The sack of Somnath in 1025 CE had made Mahmud a hero among Muslims for all time to come. "The Muslim world rang with the praises of Mahmud and he appeared to many as a great hero who had appeared upon the earth to extirpate infidelity and establish the true faith. This accounts for the legends and stories which have clustered round his name."[21] At the other end it filled Indians with a sense of shame and an urge for revenge. It was this urge that prompted the Jats to fight the foe on his return journey through the desert of Sindh. Mahmud's army suffered much in its retreat, first through the arid desert of Sindh and next through the Sindh Sagar Doab, where it was so harassed and delayed by the Jats of that region that it was not until the spring

18 For details see Lal, *The Legacy of Muslim Rule in India*, pp. 112-14.
19 Elliot's Appendix in E.D., I, p. 529.
20 Nizamuddin, Persian text, pp. 16-17; Farishtah, I, p. 35.
21 Ishwari Prasad, *Medieval India*, p. 95.

of 1026 that it reached Ghazni.[22] It was to avenge this harassment that Mahmud organized, in the autumn of that year, an expedition against the Jats. The Jats knew that Mahmud was invincible in land warfare. So they fought him on the waters of the river Jhelum. Mahmud marched to Multan and there ordered to be built a fleet of 1,400 boats each of which was furnished with archers with bows and arrows, grenades and naphtha. The Jats also had a flotilla of eight thousand boats to meet the Muslims, but they were defeated. Many of them were put to the sword.[23] "The Muslims then disembarked on the islands where the Jats had placed their wives and families for safety and carried off the women and children as slaves."[24] The Jat hatred was still more inflamed and we will meet them again and again opposing the Muslim invaders and rulers in future.

Khokhars resist Muhammad Ghauri

What the Jats did to the armies of Muhammad bin Qasim and Mahmud of Ghazni, the Khokhars did to Muhammad Ghauri's . The stronghold of the Khokhars was the Salt Range. Situated in the north of the Punjab, the Salt Range stretches from the Jhelum on the east to the Indus on the west, and crops up again beyond the latter river. Known earlier as Mokialah Hills and Koh-i-Jud, it covers Shahpur and Mianwali districts of the Punjab and (now) contains the fort of Rohtas.

Kakars, Gakkhars and Khokhars, besides many other tribes, inhabited the North-West Frontier Province, Baluchistan and the Punjab in the medieval period. The first three, however, because of similarity in nomenclature are prone to create confusion. These were three different tribes. Kakars and Gakkhars are of trans-Indus region while Khokhars are indigenous.[25] The Khokhars

---

22 C.H.I., III, pp. 25-26.

23 Nizamuddin, Persian text, pp. 16-17; Farishtah, I, p. 35.

24 C.H.I., III, p. 26. Sir Henry Elliot considers a "naval battle" rather improbable (E.D., II, Appendix, p. 477).

25 A.B.M. Habibullah, *The Foundation of Muslim Rule in India*, Appendix C, p. 369; Lal, *Twilight*, p. 85 n. 6.

were residents of or migrated to India prior to Muslim conquest. They lived mostly on both sides of the river Jhelum, but also spread in many parts of the Punjab including Sialkot and even Lahore. Today the Khokhars are split up into Muslim, Rajput and Jat sections. Originally they were all Hindus. Both Minhaj Siraj and Hasan Nizami describe them as infidels.[26] The tale of their resistance to Islam and conversion to it synchronises with the Muslim invasions of India.

The Khokhars first encountered the Muslims when Mahmud of Ghazni invaded Hindustan in 1008 CE. It was a major conflict. Anandpal of the Hindu Shahiya dynasty had decided to fight the Musalmans to the finish and expel them for good. Accordingly, says Farishtah, he invited the Rajas of Ujjain, Gwalior, Kalinjar, Kanauj, Delhi and Ajmer. They all advanced towards the Punjab with their armies. Hindu women helped furnish resources of war by selling their jewels and ornaments. The Khokhars joined in the national struggle. Hindus and Musalmans remained encamped at Waihind for forty days, neither side initiating action. Then Mahmud ordered six thousand archers to the front to spur the enemy to attack. "A force of 30,000 Khokhars, bare-headed and bare-footed and armed with strange weapons"[27] penetrated into Musalman lines where a dreadful carnage ensued resulting in the killing of 5,000 of the invaders in a few minutes. Utbi admits that the battle lasted from morning till evening and the "infidels" were near gaining victory.[28] But luck favoured Mahmud. Anandpal's elephant with the Raja on its back took to flight from Mahmud's "naphtha balls and flights of arrows", and the Indian army lost. But the contribution of the Khokhars in the battle was significant because the Shahiya dynasty now established their new capital Nandana in the Salt Range which was the country of the Khokhars held by that dynasty. After Muhammad bin Qasim's invasion, Sindh had passed into the

26 Habibullah, op.cit. p. 78 and notes 107 and 108 on p. 86.

27 Wolseley Haig in C.H.I, III, pp. 15-16.

28 *Tarikh-i-Yamini*, E.D., II, pp. 33-34; Farishtah, I, p. 26. Also Hodivala, p. 142.

hands of an Arab dynasty but the Shahiya dynasty had kept holding the Salt Range.

Later on, the Khokhars of the Salt Range made communication between Muhammad Ghauri in Ghazni and Qutbuddin Aibak in Lahore precarious and devastated Lahore in 1205 CE. When Muhammad Ghauri personally mounted his last campaign against Hindustan in 1205-06, Aibak proceeded as far as Peshawar to join him, and the two together attacked the Khokhar stronghold in the Koh-i-Jud or the Salt Range. The Hindus (Khokhars) fled to the highest in the mountains. They were pursued. Those that escaped the sword fled to the dense depth of the jungle; others were massacred or taken captive. Great plunder was obtained and many slaves "so that five Hindu [Khokhar] captives could be sold for *a dinar*".[29] Captives were so plentiful that they were also sent "to be sold in Khurasan, not long after".[30] But the Khokhars had their revenge when the Sultan was returning to Ghazni from Lahore; they formed a conspiracy to kill him. On his way he halted at Dhamyak in the Jhelum district where he was stabbed to death in March 1206.[31] Some chroniclers specifically mention Khokhars as the killers of the Sultan.[32]

According to Farishtah, three to four hundred thousand Khokhars were converted to Islam by Muhammad Ghauri,[33] but this figure is inflated. More than a hundred years later, Amir Khusrau refers to Khokhars as a non-Muslim tribe, and the way they were constantly attacked and killed by sultans Iltutmish and Balban confirms Khusrau's contention.[34] Minhaj also says that "the Khokhars were not annihilated in this affair (Muhammad-Qutbuddin attack) by any means, and gave great trouble in after years".[35]

---

29 Hasan Nizami, *Taj-ul-Massir*, E.D., II, p. 235; Minhaj, p. 484n.

30 Minhaj, p. 487n.

31 Hasan Nizami, *Taj-ul-Massir*, E.D., II, pp. 235-36; Badaoni, I, p. 79; Farishtah, I, p. 60.

32 Habibullah, op.cit. p. 78.

33 Farishtah, I, pp. 59-60.

34 Amir Khusrau, *Tughlaq Nama*, Aurangabad text, p. 128.

35 Minhaj, p. 484n.

Forests as Haven of Refugees

Mahmud Ghaznavi's invasions wrought havoc in Hindustan. There was colossal loss on every count. In the area of demography alone, according to an estimate made earlier quoting figures and facts, "during the first quarter of the eleventh century the loss of Indian population due to Mahmud's invasions was about 2,000,000,"[36] or twenty lakhs. This gives rise to a very pertinent question. If such was the dispersal and extinction of Hindu population during the invasions of Mahmud of Ghazni, how was it that the Hindus survived at all during subsequent Muslim invasions and rule spanning a period of eight hundred years? Curiously enough one reason of their survival was India's forests and rivers. These provided safe haven to the fugitives and for organising resistance by those who were determined to strike back.

In this respect as in many others, India's forests have been a boon to the country. In ancient times Hindu seers developed great philosophies in the silent and serene quietude of the jungles; in medieval times they served as green fortresses of escape and offense. While encountering the onslaughts of an aggressive and ruthless enemy, thousands and thousands of people sought shelter in the impenetrable jungles, and although in course of time they drifted into becoming "scheduled" tribes and low castes, they did manage to survive with their religion and culture. And from the jungle "fortresses" many Rajas and people dashed out to beat the enemy in offensive guerrilla attacks, offence being another form of defence.

In India's tropical climate vast stretches of hills and plains drenched by the south-west monsoons and north-east rains, used to turn into forests in the then unpolluted ecology. Forests in medieval India abounded; there were jungles throughout the country. The hills were (as they still are) covered with a stunted forest growth. In the plains thick forests spread right from Assam and Bengal to Allahabad and beyond. Both hills and forests were a boon to those who were determined to resist the Muslim invaders

---

36 See Lal, *Growth of Muslim Population in Medieval India,* pp. 211-217.

and expansion of Muslim rule in India.

To guesstimate the area covered by forests in the medieval times, it may be noted that at present India loses each year through deforesting a territory bigger than France, that is, nearly two million hectares. In 1993 about 19.47 per cent of the total geographical area of the country was actually under forest cover,[37] while in 1950 one-third of India's area was still forested. In medieval times when there was no population pressure, no big dams, no railway networks (perhaps the largest swallowers of forest land), no money-spinning saw-mills, India was covered with forests everywhere.[38] Ibn Battuta says that *gendas* (rhinoceroses) were found in the jungles of Allahabad[39] and emperor Akbar used to hunt leopards thirty to forty kms. from Agra.[40] Similarly, there were forests even in the environs of Delhi so that, during the reign of Balban, harassed Mewatis used to retaliate by issuing forth from the jungles in the immediate vicinity south-west of Delhi, attack the city, and keep the king on tenterhooks.[41]

Growth of dense forests was the cause as well as effect of heavy rains from July to September and excessively hot season in May and June. Forests received sustenance from rainfall and rains helped in the growth of forests, and both assisted in the formation of small rivulets and development of large rivers. Forests, rains and rivers all helped the freedom loving forest dwellers in maintaining their independence and culture. It is truly said that in India it does not rain, it pours. The rainfall in the north and the northeastern India — Uttar Pradesh, Bihar and Bengal, including eastern Bengal and parts of Assam (the Hindustan of medieval times) — is in the following order: the average annual rainfall in U.P., Bihar and Bengal is 100 to 200 cms. (40 to 80 inches), in eastern Bengal and Assam it is 200 to

37 *India, 1993,* Publications Division, p. 191.
38 Francois Gautier, *The Wonder that is India,* pp. 123-24.
39 Ibn Battuta, pp. 5, 111.
40 *Ain.*, I, p. 297.
41 Barani, p. 56.

400 cms. and in some parts above 400 cms. (80 to 160 and above 160 inches). In all probability a similar average obtained in the medieval period also. Medieval chroniclers do not speak in quantitative terms; in their language, "rivulets used to turn into rivers and rivers into seas during the rainy season." The situation is best depicted by the sixteenth century invader Zahiruddin Muhammad Babur in his Memoirs, *Tuzuk-i-Baburi* or *Babur Nama.* He writes about Hindustan, thus: "Sometimes it rains 10, 15, or 20 times a day, torrents pour down all at once and rivers flow where no water had been."[42] Such intensity of rainfall had rendered precarious the grip of Muslim rulers in many parts. It had helped many victims of aggression to escape into inaccessible wilds to add to the numbers of tribals and backward castes.

Reverting from this generalization to the specific instances in Mahmud Ghaznavi's time, we find that after the capture of Baran, as told by Al Utbi, the minister of Mahmud, "when he (Rai Kulchand) saw that the Sultan advanced against him ... he drew up his army and elephants *within a deep forest* ready for action."[43] Later, when Mahmud arrived in Kanauj, "many of its inhabitants were scattered abroad" and sought shelter in jungles. Chand Rai, the chief of Sarsawa near Saharanpur, "departed secretly with his property, elephants, and treasure, to the hill country, which was exceedingly lofty, *hiding himself in the jungles which the sun could not penetrate,* and concealing even the direction of his flight", to escape forcible conversion at the hands of Mahmud. Although the escapees did not always succeed, as in this case, because the Sultan pursued him by "marching fifteen parasangs through the forest, which was so thorny that the faces of his men were scarified and bloody ... he at last came to his enemy (and) many infidels were consequently slain".[44] In short, the importance of forests in defence and offence by the Hindus cannot be undernoted, even if the resisters turned from

42 *Babur Nama,* p. 519.
43 *Tarikh-i-Yamini,* E.D., II, p. 43. Emphasis added.
44 Ibid., pp. 46, 48-49. Emphasis added.

civilian city dwellers to the status of tribals.

Resistance of Hindu Low Castes to Albari Sultans

Mahmud Ghaznavi was a despot. He held his empire together by force of arms and terror.[45] Through the appointment of select Turkish generals as his viceroys in India, "whose sole business was to wage war against the Thakurs (Rais) ... Mahmud sought to make the plunder of Hindustan a permanent affair,"[46] sending many more people to starvation, to slavery and into the wilds.

From 1191 to 1193 Muhammad Ghauri attacked India again and again and, after the defeat and death of Prithviraj and Jayachandra, the whole of North India upto Varanasi became part of his empire.[47] Before this, areas from Kashmir to Gujarat were also coming under constant attacks by Muslims creating chaos and sending many people everywhere into jungles for safety. In the First Battle of Taraori fought between Muhammad Ghauri and Prithviraj, the Rajput army comprised three thousand elephants, two hundred thousand horse and a large infantry. The figures would point to large numbers of people of all castes joining in battle. Many died on the field, many others were reduced to the status of lower castes. But they did not remain quiet in their helpless state. Jats, Khokhars and Gakkars, the SCs and STs of medieval India, enthusiastically fought against foreign invaders. Meos, Minas, Katehriyas and people of the Doab fought against the Albari Sultans commonly known as the Slave Dynasty.

Thus the three-quarters of a century rule of the Albaris met with resistance not only from ruling Hindu houses, but also from Hindu lower classes whom they had sent into wilderness. Ziyauddin Barani has correctly stated the fact that the policy of

45 Bosworth, *The Ghaznavids*, p. 59. Also Muhammad Shaban, *Islamic History*, II, pp. 181-82.

46 M. Habib, *Indian Culture and Social Life at the Time of Turkish Invasions*, p. 95.

47 Fakhre Mudabbir, *Tarikh-i-Fakhruddin Mubarak Shah*, p. 23; Farishtah, I, p. 58.

the early Turkish sultans was to rule with a stern hand, and to crush all opposition by instilling terror into the hearts of the people in general and the rebels in particular.[48] He also correctly diagnosed that the result of this policy was to make the people flee to and hide in the jungles.[49] There, with time, their numbers grew. There they somehow eked out an existence, for life in the forests was hard. There their hearts were filled with bitterness so that whenever they found a chance they sneaked out from their hilly or forest retreats and waylaid Muslim travellers on highways. They targeted important persons in particular. For instance, when Bahram Shah defeated his sister Sultan Raziyah (1236-40) and her husband Altuniah at Kaithal, and they fell into the hands of Hindu peasants, the latter put them to death.[50] In short, the Hindus living in the wilds defied the authority of the Sultanate and committed "highway robbery". Muslim chroniclers often refer to them as "robbers". But in fact they were peasants turned jungle-dwellers turned guerrilla warriors who were not easy to control.

Consequently, a great offensive was launched against Minas and Meos of Mewat during the reign of Sultan Nasiruddin. Mewat is the ill-defined tract lying south of Delhi and including parts of Mathura and Gurgaon districts, most of Alwar and a little of old Bharatpur state. It takes its name from Meos who were originally the same as Minas of Rajputana. In 1259, Sultan Nasiruddin's Prime Minister Ulugh Khan (later Sultan Balban) undertook an expedition against the hilly country of Mewat where Hindu rebels used to plunder the property of Muslims and sack villages in Haryana, Siwalik and Bayana. Ulugh Khan had marched to chastise them three years earlier also. In 1259 they had once again gathered under their Hindu leader Malka. Ulugh Khan defeated them and treated them most cruelly. He put nearly

---

48 Barani, pp. 31-34, 47.

49 Ibid., pp. 56, 473-74.

50 Minhaj, Text, pp. 190, 192; Isami, *Futuh-us-Salatin*, trs. Mahdi Husain, II, p. 263; Nizamuddin, I, p. 68.

12,000 of them to the sword, enslaved 250 of their leaders and seized much booty in cash and horse. The Mewatis did not forget this treatment and burnt with rage for revenge. When Ulugh Khan ascended the throne as Sultan Balban, they resumed their operations. Whenever they found it opportune, during day or night, they raided the capital city of Delhi or came prowling into it. They assaulted the water-carriers (*bhishtis*) at the Hauz-i-Shamsi, molested the girls who came to fetch water, and stripped them of their clothes. This was not the work of Rajas or Zamindars but of the forest dwellers whom the policy of the Sultan had sent into desperation or who on their own had taken the offensive. To meet the menace, the Sultan cleared the jungles and defeated them, but it took a whole year to stamp out their depredations,[51] and cost the Sultan a hundred thousand soldiers. Balban built strong outposts and garrisoned them with ferocious Afghans, but the Mewatis could not be completely crushed, not even after "Alauddin Khilji made a minar on the skulls of 30,000 Meos to dissuade them from sacking Delhi".[52] During years and centuries of Muslim government's pressure, many Meos were converted to Islam. Muslim Meos are known as Mewatis. But whether Hindu or Musalman, they kept up their traditional resistance. The converted Mewatis have preserved many Hindu customs, such as exogamous marriage rules and observance of Hindu festivals.

Similarly in the Doab, in Kampil, Patiali, and Bhojpur there were strongholds of "robbers" who infested the roads and rendered impossible the movement of merchants and travellers. The Sultan proceeded in person to quell these disorders and posted strong Afghan garrisons to put down "brigandage and lawlessness". The Delhi sultans did not hesitate to call Afghans from outside to crush people in Hindustan; the people of the wilds did not

51 Barani, pp. 56-57.

52 Ashim Gill, 'Mixed yet pure: Meos who pride themselves more as Kshatriyas than Muslim' in an article in the Sunday Magazine of *The Hindustan Times*, August 11, 1995, quoting Dr. Jaweeed Ashraf of the Jawaharlal Nehru University, New Delhi.

cease attacking the Muslim merchants and wayfarers. After the Sultan had cleared the jungles in the neighbourhood of Delhi, he gave the towns and country within the Doab to some distinguished chiefs with directions to lay waste and destroy the villages of "the marauders, to slay the men, to make prisoners of women and children, to clear away the jungles, and to suppress all unlawful proceedings".[53] Later on, the Sultan himself proceeded to the neighbourhood of Kampil and Patiali. "He remained there for five or six months putting the rebels to the sword." Ziyauddin Barani writes that "the den of the robbers was thus converted into a guard-house, and Musalmans and guardians of the way took the place of highway robbers,"[54] which means that the local Hindus were exiled and Muslims settled in their place.

While Sultan Balban was thus engaged in suppressing insurgency in the Doab, news arrived from Katehar that disturbances had broken out there. The Katehriya Rajputs' "mutiny" extended to Badaon and Amroha. These Rajputs and their lower caste followers acquired such strength that the chiefs of Badaon and Amroha were unable to keep order and were landed in great trouble. Balban crossed the river Ganga after "marching for two nights and three days". He sent forward 5,000 archers to burn down Katehar and destroy it, to slay every man, and to spare none but women and children, "not even boys who had reached the age of eight or nine years". In the Katehar region "woodcutters were sent into the jungles to cut roads, and road making proved more efficacious in establishing order than punitive expeditions". But Barani repeats a similar statement in his narrative of Alauddin Khalji's reign, which means that despite Balban's draconian measures, the trouble continued as before.[55] Balban remained in Katehar for some days and directed the slaughter. Heaps of the slain were to be seen near every village and jungle. The

53 Barani, p. 57.
54 Ibid., p. 59.
55 Ishwari Prasad, *Medieval India*, pp. 178-79.

whole district was ravaged, and so much plunder was obtained that the royal army was enriched.

Sultan Balban next resolved upon leading a similar campaign to the mountains of Jud or the Salt Range, the stronghold of the Khokhars. The need to do so must have arisen because of the activities of these ever restive mountain people. He marched thither with a suitable force, chastised the inhabitants, and plundered the country. Many men and horses were captured; the price of the latter among soldiers fell to forty *tankahs* each.

In these fire-fighting operations, the peasants and the tribals were not always defenders against the cruel regime. They sometimes forestalled the aggressors and challenged their authority. However, the outcome of their defensive or offensive action against strong armies was the same — their flight into the jungles. There their castes, their nomenclatures and their numbers increased. Some even fled the country. Muslim invaders and rulers used to send many enslaved Hindus to Muslim lands in the west. Many hardpressed Hindus migrated to the east on their own. They escaped to as far off regions as the hills of Nepal right from the twelfth century onwards.[56]

56 *Gazetteer of Afghanistan and Nepal*, pp. 108-109.

IV
Growth of Tribes and Castes Under Muslim Rule

In the foregoing pages it has been seen that Hindu tribes and lower castes, along with their Rajas, resisted the onslaughts of Muslim invaders and sultans. If they found the invader too strong or the sultan or amir too cruel, they fled their homes and sought shelter in jungle and mountain hideouts. This process of flight continued throughout the medieval period resulting in the birth and growth of new tribes and castes and rise in the numbers of the existing ones with whom the fugitives intermingled. In the early years they escaped into the wilds on the approach of an alien army or when they lost in battle against it. They also escaped to avoid living under the discriminatory regulations of Muslim rule. But this could be done only by the daring and the desperate. The majority of the people stayed on in the countryside as zimmis. "Zimmis are not citizens of the Muslim state ... but are suffered to live on payment of poll tax Jaziyah." In return they are entitled to protection of life.[1]

Besides the fortunes of war, there were many other occasions and reasons for people to move out of their settled abodes. Sometimes Muslim sultans used to order exile of the people whom they considered undesirable. Jalaluddin Khalji exiled some "Thugs" and "highwaymen" from Delhi and Alauddin Khalji turned out vintners and wine sellers from the capital city. Many people must have escaped into the jungles during the long march from Delhi to Devagiri when Muhammad bin Tughlaq shifted his capital to the Deccan.[2] Capital of Hindustan was also changed from Delhi to Agra by Sikandar Lodi and from Agra

1 Aghnides, *Muhammadan Theories of Finance*, pp. 399, 528; *Encyclopaedia of Islam*, I, pp. 958-59.

2 Barani, pp. 472, 479-84.

back to Delhi by Shahjahan. Deserters who fled the army, say during the Gujarat campaign of Alauddin[3] or the Thatta campaign under Firoz Tughlaq,[4] would have either sought shelter with some Hindu Raja but more likely would have escaped into some inaccessible hideouts. During famines or when there was acute scarcity of water, the people left their homes for whatever place they thought could provide relief.[5] Foreign attacks and disturbances at home (*fitna*) also saw people fleeing their homes for shelter elsewhere. Sometimes new cities were founded and their old residents expelled as a matter of punishment. Abdul Qadir Badaoni, writing in the reign of Akbar, says that Sher Shah in the year of his accession "laid waste the city of Qannauj, and moving it from its original site re-established it on the banks of the river Ganges; it is now known as Shergarh. In the same manner he destroyed the fortress of Shamsabad and removed it to another place, calling it by the name of Rasulpur." He also "destroyed" the old cities of Delhi founded by Alauddin Khalji and Humayun and built new structures and a new surrounding wall.[6] Firozabad town in Agra district was destroyed and rebuilt in the sixteenth century by a eunuch named Malik Firoz, under orders of Akbar, because Todar Mal was insulted by the inhabitants.[7] Similarly, Aurangabad Saiyyad, a town in Bulandshahr district, was founded in 1704 by one Saiyyad Abdul Aziz, who undertook, with the permission of emperor Aurangzeb, to eject the turbulent Jaroliyas of the neighbourhood.[8] Such expulsion-motivated foundations of cities apart, urbanization went on throughout Muslim rule with ardent zeal and so also migrations of "undesirable people" into uninhabited regions.

But in all such situations mentioned above, the migration

3 Isami, pp. 244-46; Yahiya, p. 76; Hajiuddabir, *Zafar-ul-Walih*, p. 790.
4 Afif, pp. 224-25. For detailed references, Ishwari Prasad, *Medieval India*, pp. 302-303.
5 Barani, pp. 568, 571-72.
6 Badaoni, I, p. 472.
7 *Imp. Gaz.*, United Provinces of Agra and Oudh, I, p. 416.
8 Ibid., p. 345.

was not necessarily into forests. Besides, it was neither large nor permanent in nature. The largest numbers who escaped into the jungles and stayed there were helpless agriculturists. Often the Muslim regime exploited them to the fullest extent, sucked them dry through excessive taxation, and treated them so cruelly during collection or default in payment that they were left with no option but to flee into the jungles. They left their lands, escaped into jungles, and did nor return because of fear of reprisals — except of course some of the daring sort, called "bandits" by Muslim chroniclers.[9] They made forests and similar hideouts their permanent abode, swelling the ranks of what today are called Scheduled Tribes, Scheduled Castes and Other Backward Castes.

Under the Turks

Muslim rule in Hindustan was established in about 1200 CE. During the next two hundred years it was entrenched under the Slave, the Khalji and the Tughlaq dynasties and its administration systematized. The greatest king of the Sultanate period was Alauddin Khalji (1296-1316). He introduced a number of measures and reforms in Muslim administration. He was an imperialist and his conquests were extensive. His main source of strength was the army.[10] His grand army consisted of 4,75,000 horsemen and a large body of infantry[11] and he made the agriculturists pay for its maintenance — salary of soldiers, construction and maintenance of forts, manufacture of weapons and engines of war. The Muslim rulers lived in luxury. They spent lavishly. All expenses of the government, on the army, on administration, on construction of palaces, mosques, tombs and other buildings, on payment of awards and pensions to Muslims — men of letters and men of religion —, on the harems of royalty and nobility etc., were borne by the peasants. It is true that the main source of revenue in the medieval times was agriculture. It is also true

9 Barani, p. 443.
10 Barani, p. 102. See also his *Fatawa-i-Jahandari*, p. 22.
11 Barani, pp. 303, 323-24; Afif, p. 283.

that there were no budgets prepared by governments to adjust income and expenditure, that there was no difference between the state treasury and the king's privy purse, and that he collected taxes as he liked and spent the money as he chose. But Alauddin Khalji collected every possible penny from the cultivators, leaving them a bare minimum for their own subsistence. His aims were two — to collect maximum amount of taxes to pay for the expenses of the government and also to impoverish the people in order to cripple them economically and politically. His motives were also two — political and religious

Alauddin used to be kept correctly informed by his counsellors and ulema on the Islamic law with regard to the treatment to be meted out to the non-Muslims in the Muslim state. The Shariat law suited his needs and aims immensely. It helped him to keep the "recalcitrant" Hindus humiliated and suppressed. People's resistance to Muslim rule was continual, and Alauddin and his advisers arrived at the conclusion that it was "wealth" which provided motivation and sinews of rebellion and disaffection. The people, therefore, must be impoverished. The Sultan resorted to draconian measures and "directed that only so much (of the produce) be left with his subjects (*raiyyat*) as would maintain them from year to year ... without admitting of their having articles in excess". The Sultan ordered collection of fifty per cent of the agricultural produce as land tax; besides he imposed house tax, grazing tax and many other cesses. As if this burden was not enough, he also collected the *jizyah*. *Jizyah* had the religious connotation of humiliating the Hindus. Its incidence was also very heavy. The sultans of Delhi charged ten, twenty, and forty (silver) *tankahs* as *jizyah* from the poor, the middle class and the rich respectively.[12]

If the burden of taxes was heavy, the method of collection was humiliating. Ziyauddin Barani says that Alauddin Khalji preferred to collect land revenue in kind.[13] So also was the preference

12 Afif, p. 383.
13 Barani, pp. 305-307.

of Ibrahim Lodi. It means that most of the sultans found it convenient to collect the revenue in kind. Assessment was done on cash basis but collection was done in kind. The main reason was that there was hardly any cash found with peasants to pay revenue with. In medieval chronicles, gold, silver, precious stones and minted money are mentioned as urban phenomenon associated with kings, nobles, *sahukars* and merchants.[14] The presence of a silver coin was a rare sight in the village. Abdullah writes clearly that as there was acute shortage of cash during the reign of Ibrahim Lodi, he ordered his officers to collect revenue in kind.[15] In the payment of revenue by the peasant to his superior — *muqaddam, chaudhari, zamindar* (these three are synonymous) — or by the *muqaddam* to the *iqtadar*, or by the peasant or *zamindar* to the assignee of land, the process of payment was in kind.

What payment in kind actually meant is most significant. Today taxes are paid through bank drafts or cheques or currency notes. And although the pinch of payment might be felt, no humiliation is experienced in the process of payment. But payment in kind, say of land revenue, was very different in nature. It meant either of the two things. One, that when the crop got ready for harvesting, the revenue collectors arrived with retainers or retinues of troops, cut the government's share of the crop and took it away. Later the cultivators cut their share or whatever was left of it. The other was that the cultivators cut the whole crop, stored it in bags, and when government collectors arrived, they took away the government's share leaving a bare minimum with the peasant for his sustenance. Visualize either of the two situations; there was bound to be resentment and a possibility of conflict in most cases. A peasant and his family or a group of peasants and their families go through all the hard work of producing the grain and piling it up, say in a hundred bags, and then

---

14 Ibid., pp. 99, 118, 130, 223, 228, 251-52, 262, 284, 333. Once one lakh *tankahs* were awarded to a noble, p.203. There were also *tankahs* of gold, p. 280; Afif, pp. 74, 248, 264.

15 Abdullah, p. 105.

the government collectors descend on the village and take away fifty to seventy bags as land revenue and other sundry taxes. Take away, because it is human nature that no one is happy to part with a major share of his hard-earned produce. Take away, because the tax collectors were always accompanied by armed men.[16] It was the duty of the *shiqdar* to assist with troops the *amils* in collection of land revenue and other taxes. In many cases the batch of collectors were no better than raiding parties and the cultivators resisted them. Everyone in those days carried arms. The *shiqdar's* men came with swords and lances; the peasants possessed axes, clubs and staffs mounted with spikes, if nothing more sophisticated, and often gave a good fight. The collectors abused and kicked, delivered *lathi*-blows, squeezed with pincers and tongs, chained and sometimes even incarcerated the peasants.[17] Sometimes even one armed soldier or revenue collector demanding *kharaj* used to put "rope round the necks of twenty *zamindars*, *muqaddams* and *chaudharis*, kick them and lash them with rods".[18] Some *zamindars* could not put up with such humiliation. For example, during the period when Jalaluddin Khalji was the *Naib* of Samana and *Iqtadar* of Kaithal, a village of the Mandahar (Rajputs) of that area was sacked by his men. At this the Mandahar Zamindar rushed straight upon Jalaluddin, struck him with drawn sword, and inflicted two such severe cuts across his face that their scars remained for the rest of his life.[19] But such violent reactions were not always possible.

In short, utmost strictness was practised by *amils* and *karkuns* in collecting *kharaj* and all other taxes. Because the government officials who could not collect the taxes in full were themselves punished with "kicks, pincers (*shikanja*), bindings,

---

16 Every noble had his contingents. For example, the *Iqtadar* of Kanod and Jubala possessed a contigent of 700 horse. Malik Qabul Ulugh Khan was given large *iqtas* and contingents of cavalry and infantry to enfore Market Regulation under Alauddin Khalji (Barani, pp. 204, 305-6, 402).

17 Barani, pp. 183, 315-18, 385; Afif, pp. 37-38.

18 Barani, p. 288.

19 Ibid., pp. 194-195.

blows and incarcerations".[20] The Department of *Mustakhraj* was entrusted with the task of inquiring into the arrears lying in the names of collectors (*amils*, *amins*, *karkuns*), and realizing them.[21] The result was that tax collectors behaved most callously and "if one *amil* left one cow with the peasant, another used to take away that also".[22]

There were varied reactions to such harsh and rigorous measures. The contemporary chronicler Ziyauddin Barani writes that "the Hindus" were impoverished to such an extent that there was no sign of gold and silver left with them and the wives of *khuts* and *muqaddams* used to seek jobs in the houses of the Musalmans, work there and receive wages.[23] In the time of Alauddin's uncle, Sultan Jalaluddin, these Hindus used to dress in white, ride horses and move about among the Musalmans with comfort and ease.[24] Such people could not have been reduced to extremities even in the time of Alauddin, in spite of his cruel and harsh orders. In this situation, *khuts* and *muqaddams* and *zamindars* who possessed the strength to defy, never cared for the revenue officers and avoided payment of taxes "by way of *kharaj*, *jizyah*, *kari* and *charai*".[25]

Most Zamindars and peasants, however, paid the taxes meekly. They lived in peace but not in permanent peace nor with much honour. Kings, nobles, *iqtadars* and assignees changed so often that sometimes the peasant was made to pay *kharaj* twice in the course of a single year. Pressure of *kharaj* was put on big Zamindars to gain political ends or matrimonial alliances.[26] Besides, looting of crops when ready was a fashion with marching armies resulting in acute shortage among the people.[27] In short,

20 Ibid., p. 431.
21 Ibid., pp. 288-92. Also see Tripathi, *Some Aspects of Muslim Administration*, p. 262.
22 Afif, p. 98.
23 Barani, p. 288.
24 Ibid., pp. 216-17.
25 Ibid., p. 291.
26 Afif, pp. 37-38.
27 Afif, pp. 205-206, 232-33; Barani, pp. 446, 450.

the position of the *muqaddams* and peasants who paid their dues to live in peace was not all that good. They worked out in the fields round the year. They had to perform the task of patrolling the roads and guiding travellers with lighted torches. But the *kharaj* the cultivator must pay, sometimes even by selling his wife and children.[28] If he resisted, he invariably failed against the superior forces of the regime.[29] As a last resort he fled and sought refuge in secluded places like hills and dales and forests and joined the ranks of what today are called scheduled tribes and backward castes. Those who fled into the forests included all groups of people — Rajas defeated in battle, Zamindars unable to pay taxes, and pauperized peasants.[30]

Ghiyasuddin Tughlaq also more or less followed the policy of Alauddin Khalji. His instructions to the revenue officers were that "there should be left only so much to the Hindus that neither on the one hand should they become intoxicated on account of their wealth, nor on the other should they become so destitute as to leave their lands and cultivation in despair".[31] Muhammad Tughlaq's army was 900,000, double the size of that of Alauddin.[32] His enhancement of land revenue and consequent hardships to the peasants are too well-known to need a repetition. The principle of leaving the "bare minimum" to the peasantry became the norm of Muslim rule as such. It was not confined to the Sultanate period only but, as we shall see, was projected to the Mughal period also.

The Hindus in revenge used to set fire to the harvest (*khirman*) of foodgrains, reduce them to ashes and drive away the animals and flee from homes. The Sultan ordered the *shiqdars* and *faujdars* to sack and loot. Some *muqaddams* and *zamindars* were executed;

28 Barani, p. 340.

29 Siddiqi, *Some Aspects of Afghan Despotism in India*, Aligarh, 1969, p. 160.

30 Afif, pp. 161-62, 172, 210-212.

31 Barani, p. 430.

32 Al Umri, *Masalik-ul-Absar*, E.D., III, p. 576; Al-Qalqashindi, *Subh-ul-Asha*, p. 66.

some others were blinded. Those who managed to escape used to "join together and hide themselves in the jungles", and the countryside used to be ruined. During the days the Sultan was in Baran, he ordered that the whole region should be ravaged. "People brought heads of Hindus" and those who escaped sought shelter in the forests as usual.[33]

Ibn Battuta gives a description of this phenomenon. "The Muslims dominate the infidels," writes he, "but the latter fortify themselves in mountains, in rocky, uneven and rugged places as well as in bamboo groves (or clusters). Here bamboos are not hollow. [Battuta refers to male bamboo poles called *balli*]. Their stems are so inextricably intertwined that even fire has no effect on them, they cannot be burnt down and they are very strong. The *kafirs* take residence in these jungles and these forests become like ramparts (or forts) for them, as it were. They collect rainwater. They have their fields tilled and animals pastured there. That is why they cannot be subdued except (through the induction of) large armies. Soldiers (of the Sultan) enter the jungles and cut down the bamboos with instruments especially crafted for the purpose."[34]

But Muslim soldiers were not always successful. For, Amir Timur, writing in his *Mulfuzat* more than half a century later, noted that one of the important defences of Hindustan "consists of woods and forests and trees, which intertwining stem with stem and branch with branch render it very difficult to penetrate the country". And "the soldiery, the landlords and Princes, and Rajas of that country, who inhabit fastnesses in those forests, (though) live there like wild beasts", organize resistance.[35]

Amir Khusrau, Barani and Ibn Battuta all speak of Hindu inhabitants concealing themselves in jungles. Amir Timur's statement adds two significant dimensions to the scenario. One

---

33 Barani, pp. 473, 479-80, 483-84.

34 Ibn Battuta, p. 124; Hindi trs. by Rizvi in *Tughlaq Kalin Bharat*, I, p. 238. Also Utbi, *Tarikh-i-Yamini*, E.D., II, pp. 49-50.

35 Sharfuddin Yazdi, *Zafar Nama*, II, pp. 168-69; *Mulfuzat-i-Timuri*, E.D., III, p. 395; Mir Khwand, *Rauzat-us-Safa*, VI, p. 116.

is that Princes and Rajas also used to escape into the forests and reside in fastnesses there. The second is that life there was very hard and they lived like wild beasts. Jungles were the fittest place for the Rajas to escape to because their men were familiar with the terrain while the sultan's army was not accustomed to manoeuvring in the forests.[36] Urban Muslims — kings and nobles and even troops — were scared of jungles where strong resisters lurked in the shadow of every tree.

So, by the time of Timur (c. 1400) it was well known that not only harassed agriculturists but also defeated Rajas and helpless Zamindars sought refuge in the forests. Those who took to the jungle, stayed there, eating wild fruits, tree roots, and the coarsest grain if and when available, but surely preserving their freedom. With the passing of time these people became tribals living the life of beasts.

All Muslim chroniclers, without exception, whether writing in Arabic or Persian, from the time of Arab invasion of Sindh to the sixteenth century and beyond, make mention about the escape of the people of Hindustan into the jungles. But they all speak about the phenomenon in general terms. They nowhere mention the numbers of people who sought refuge in the forests and wilds nor do they name the forests to which they fled. How many refugees were Rajas or Zamindars and how many were peasants or people of other categories? How many belonged to the upper castes and how many to the lower castes? How many sought shelter in the forests as a consequence of Muslim invasions or cruelty of Muslim rulers and governors, and how many to escape the oppressive tax laws? These questions remain unanswered by the chroniclers. However, they only make mention of the flight of people into the forests, not of any returnees. If there was only immigration into the jungles and no emigration, then the number of forest dwellers would have gone on increasing with the passage of time. This indeed seems to be so, looking to their numbers today. The refugees would have 'converted' to the

36 Afif, pp. 172, 210-12.

classes and cadres of tribes already living therein and adopted their names, or they would have formed new tribes with new names on their own. The latter assumption may be more correct. In Hindu society intermingling and admixture of castes and tribes is not easy; formation of new castes and classes by collections of new endogamous groups is the general trend. That is how there are more than 2300 SCs and STs in India today. But about this assumption no written evidence is available in Muslim chronicles.

Medieval Muslim writers, however, in the course of their narratives of political events, do sometimes refer to the activities of Rajas and peasants in the forests of their refuge. For one thing, the fugitive Rajas, as far as possible, kept contact with their compatriots outside. They despatched warning signals of impending attacks and, if possible, provided succour to them.[37] For another, they, with their followers, infested the highways near their hideouts, and waylaid Muslim merchants, in particular important government officials and caravans. This was also necessitated by the need to replenish their stock of grain and other necessaries which were scarce in the forests. This scarcity made them live like wild beasts for which they were not prepared. For their activities the Muslim chronicles dub them as "robbers", but for the people of the forests it was a struggle for existence. Their guerrilla wars were waged for self-defence, sustenance and revenge.

Their activities invited reprisals from the Muslim regime. From the beginning of Muslim rule in India, the sultans of Delhi had begun to consider themselves as the rulers of the whole of Hindustan, every Raja and Zamindar as their vassal, and every one else as their subject people. Any opposition on any one's part was considered as "rebellion". On the other hand, the people, in particular those safely entrenched in the environs of forests, were determined to defy. At least they were not easy to subdue. So, the sacking of their hideouts was never given up.

37 Utbi, *Tarikh-i-Yamini*, E.D., II, p. 48; Amir Khusrau, *Khazain-ul-Futuh*, Habib trs., pp. 51-52; Lal, *Khaljis*, pp. 234-36, 251, 253, 256, 291-92.

The result was that resistance used to push more and more people into the jungles. The cycle of resistance and repression went apace and the number of forest people went on increasing.

Under the Afghans

From after the invasion of Timur to the middle of the sixteenth century, that is, for one hundred and fifty years the Afghans dominated the history of the Sultanate. They were in a way saviours of Muslim rule. They had come in large numbers with Mahmud of Ghazni and Muhammad Ghauri. They were invited by Balban to man difficult outposts. The Saiyyad rulers in particular, invited them in droves to maintain themselves on the throne. From 1451 to 1526 CE the Lodi Afghans ruled as full fledged sultans on their own. The Sur Afghans rose to power in the wake of Humayun's exit from India in 1540 and were ousted by Akbar after the Second Battle of Panipat in 1556.

During this period (c. 1400-1556) the Sultanate of Delhi was no longer the imperial power that it was in the days of the Khaljis and the Tughlaqs. In extent it was the largest compared with the other kingdoms into which the empire had broken up, but it was not the strongest of them. Kingdoms like Jaunpur, Gujarat, Malwa, Mewar, the Bahmani and Vijayanagar were equally strong if not more. But except for Mewar and Vijayanagar, all others were Muslim states, run on the pattern of the Sultanate and in accordance with Islamic law and traditions.

The rule of the Saiyyad dynasty lasted for about thirty seven years, from 1414 to 1451. Its rulers were Khizr Khan, Mubarak Khan and the latter's successors Muhammad and Alauddin Alam Shah.

Khizr Khan's sultanate comprised of Delhi, Punjab, Sindh and Uttar Pradesh. But no region was quite submissive. The reason for recalcitrance and rebellion was the utter humiliation with which the fundamentalist Firoz Tughlaq had treated important Rajas and Zamindars like Rai Vir Singh of Gwalior, his younger brother Rawat Uddharan Singh, Rai Sumer of Etawah, and Rai Ranvir Vahan of Mainpuri. For example, Firoz Tughlaq had marched against Sumer and Uddharan in 1377-78; they with their families were taken to Delhi and forced to reside there. In the royal court they were made to sit behind Muslim nobles, not like them on a carpet but on the bare ground.[38] They had put up with this insult during the reign of Firoz, but now finding the Sultanate weak, they not only declared independence but also occupied some Sarkari *parganas* in the environment.[39]

Katehar was always turbulent and "two risings are described in the middle of the thirteenth century". In 1379 or 1380 Khargu, a Hindu chief of Katehar, murdered Saiyad Muhammad, the governor at a feast; and Firoz Tughlaq, foiled in his attempt to seize Khargu who fled to Kumaon, appointed an Afghan governor to Sambhal with orders "to invade the country of Katehar every year, to commit every kind of ravage and devastation, and not to allow it to be inhabited until the murderer was given up".[40] How many fled with Khargu to the hills and forests of Kumaon and how many more fled later into the wilds and became tribals due to Afghan pressure can better be imagined than computed.

In 1418, under the Saiyyads, the Wazir Taj-ul-Mulk marched to Katehar. Viram Singh laid waste his countryside and escaped with his men into the forest surrounding Aonla in the Kumaon hills.[41] Unable to achieve his objective of collecting revenue and tribute, the Wazir "contended himself with the ignoble but customary satisfaction of plundering the people".[42] Similar in nature was his raid on Etawah.[43] Early in 1421 Khizr Khan himself marched into Mewat. Many Mewatis escaped into the mountains while the others made their submission. Throughout the Saiyyad dynasty's rule, the yearly collection of revenue looked like raids

---

38 Afif, p. 281; Yahiya, pp. 133-34; Farishtah, I, p. 148; Hajiuddabir, *Zafar-ul-Walih*, IV, p. 898.

39 Yahiya, pp. 172-73.

40 *Imp. Gaz.*, United Provinces of Agra and Oudh, I, pp. 244-45.

41 Yahiya, p. 187; Farishtah, I, p. 162.

42 C.H.I., III, p. 207.

43 Yahiya, p. 191; Farishtah, I, p. 162; Nizamuddin, I, pp. 268-69; Badaoni, Ranking, I, p. 379.

of robber bands rather than tax-collecting officials' endeavours. It exasperated the local chiefs and Zamindars, rendered the state unsure of a regular revenue,[44] and filled the neighbouring forests with refugees.

In December 1422, beginning of the year 1423, and again in the winter of 1424, Mubarak Shah marched into Katehar. The Sultan plundered the countryside as far as Kumaon foothills and compelled Rai Har Singh to pay three years' revenue and tribute.[45] Between the long struggle between Jaunpur and Delhi kings, the former held Katehar for a time. The last revolt of the Katehariyas is said to have taken place in 1555-56.[46] Under the Mughals, the Afghans made many settlements in the Katehar region and other parts of Northern India; but they were generally soldiers of fortune rather than politicians or men of influence.[47]

The Mewatis, habitually addicted to rebellion, were up in arms again, and when the Sultan marched into Mewat, they destroyed their effects, fled to the mountains of Tijara, their stronghold.[48] Their scorched earth policy rendered pursuit difficult and the Sultan returned to Delhi in June 1425. When he visited the region again, the grandson of Bahadur Nahar repeated the tactics of laying waste their country and retired into the hill fortress of Indur. Later they proceeded to Alwar in Rajasthan.[49]

The Rajas and Zamindars of U.P. also avoided payment of tribute. Rai Sumer's son Deva Rai stoutly defended his town of Etawah when the Sultan's commander besieged it in 1423. In Uttar Pradesh also lived the Bachgotis who were a tribe of restive Rajputs descended from the Mainpuri Chauhans.[50] Now called Basgotis, they are still found in large numbers in the

44 Pringle Kennedy, *The History of the Great Mughals*, I, p. 85.

45 Yahiya, pp. 200-203; Nizamuddin, I, p. 275; Farishtah, I, p. 165.

46 *Imp. Gaz.*, United Provinces of Agra and Oudh, I, p. 245.

47 loc. cit.

48 Yahiya, p. 204; Hodivala, p. 405.

49 Powlett, *Gazetteer of Alwar*, pp. 134-35. Indur was a Mahal in the Sarkar of Tijara, *Ain.*, II, p. 192.

50 Elliot, *Races of North Western Province*, I, pp. 47-49; Badaoni, Ranking, I, pp. 414-15 and n. 13.

Allahabad-Jaunpur region. As a consequence of the persistent resistance of Zamindars against the weak Saiyyad government, Bachgoti, Baghela and Tomar Rajputs grew powerful and consolidated their small kingdoms.

This was the situation when the Lodi Afghans gradually secured control of the Sultanate of Delhi. The leader of the Bachgotis was Juga. He drove out Mubarak Khan, governor of Kara and killed his brother Sher Khan. The Baghela Raja Bhedchandra of Bhatgora (Rewa) cooperated with the Bachgotis in their resistance. Sikandar Lodi attacked them in 1493 and cut many of them down. But Juga with many followers managed to escape. Next year, 1494-95, Sikander Lodi started to deal with Raja Bhedchandra. Not much is known about the early history of this house. It appears that after the extinction of the Baghela rule in Gujarat by Alauddin Khalji in 1299, a branch of Baghela or Vaghela Rajputs with their Raja Karan sought shelter with Raja Ram Chandra of Devagiri, while the rest of the Baghelas quitted Gujarat *en masse* and settled down in the region round Banda and Kalinjar. About two centuries later their chieftain Viram Deva was so hard pressed by the Muslim rulers of Kalpi and Jaunpur that his successor Bhedchandra moved to the country now called Baghelkhand bounded by the Kaimur ranges on the north and north-west and by the Maikal ranges on the south and south-west. According to the sixteenth century Sanskrit epic *Vīrabhānūdaya* of Madhava,[51] Bhedchandra extended his authority up to Gaya in South Bihar.[52] His capital was Bandhogarh. He created trouble for the Lodis during Lodi-Sharqi war and the revolt of the Bachgotis. Sultan Sikander Lodi launched a campaign against Bagelkhand in 1495.

On arrival in the country, the Sultan was confronted by Varaharaya Deva (Bir Singh Deo of Persian chronicles), son of Bhedchandra. The Prince was defeated and forced to vacate his

51 It has been translated in abridgement by Hiranand Shastri in the Archaeological Survey of India, Memoir No. 21, 1925.

52 Archaeological Survey of India, Memoir, No. 21, p. 6.

capital. The Sultan so ravaged the countryside that on the one hand he himself was forced to retreat because of the scarcity caused by his own wanton destruction,[53] and on the other thousands of native inhabitants fled into the wilds. Varaharaya Deva with his people fled towards the forests of Sarguja and Chota Nagpur. It is no wonder that Sarguja and Chota Nagpur, considered safe refuge by pressured Rajas in the fifteenth century, are now counted as centers of Scheduled Tribes and other 'wild' clans.

Lakshmi Chand, another son of Bhedchandra, continued the struggle. Meanwhile Sikandar Lodi won over Salivahan, brother and successor of Bhedchandra. But Sikandar's original plan was to annex the kingdom. Therefore, three years later, in 1499, he attacked Salivahan for refusing to give him a daughter in marriage. He failed in his mission and so laid waste the country up to Banda.[54] The Raja of Bandhogarh continued to rule independently but with crippled strength and prosperity. In 1527 its Raja Bir Singh joined the camp of Rana Sanga against Babur at the Battle of Kanuah.

The Tomar Rajputs of Gwalior also resisted the Lodi onslaughts with equal tenacity and with the same consequences—flight into the jungles. Sikandar Lodi's intentions were expansionist. His chroniclers specifically mention that the policy of the Lodi sultans was aimed at the domination of Muslims and subordination of Hindus.[55] He was determined to annex the kingdom of Gwalior. From the year 1500 till the time of his death he strove towards that end. Although Gwalior could be taken only after Sikandar's death by his son and successor Ibrahim Lodi,[56] Sikandar himself wrought havoc in the region. He turned many habitable areas into barren lands and forced many people to become forest dwellers.

---

53 Niamatullah, fol. 56-57; Nizamuddin, I, p. 319; Farishtah I, p. 181.

54 *Imp. Gaz.*, Central India, p. 406.

55 Rizqullah, fol. 40 a; *Epigraphia Indica — Arabic and Persian Supplement*, 1959-60, p. 8.

56 For details see Lal, *Twilight*, pp. 173-84, 205-206.

The story of the extinction of the Gwalior kingdom needs to be told in some detail because, while the consequences of destruction are easy to narrate, the sequential effects on society and culture as a whole are not easy to comprehend. These can be amply understood in the history of Gwalior in the fifteenth-sixteenth century. From 1501 to 1505 Sikandar Lodi sacked Dholpur, a dependency of Gwalior, so thoroughly that trees and orchards extending to fourteen miles around were "torn up from roots". Houses and temples were destroyed and mosques built with their debris.[57] Four years later, the fort of Mandrael, standing close to river Chambal, was taken and pillaged. Indiscriminate killing and destruction resulted in the outbreak of "typhus and other bad diseases", and many of his men lost their lives. Local population was similarly affected and those who could flee escaped into nearby jungles.

In his keenness to take Gwalior as soon as possible, Sikandar Lodi shifted his capital from Delhi to Agra in 1504 so that places near Gwalior like Bayana, Dholpur, Narwar, Avantgarh etc. could be brought under control first. For this purpose he embarked on what he called *jihād*,[58] and for a whole year he fought and destroyed in the region. Another year was spent on starving Narwar into submission (1507-08), but not before the garrison had left the citadel with their belongings for the nearby forest. We know from Abul Fazl that a thick forest existed near Narwar. "From the closeness of the trees and the thickness of the branches, it was difficult...to penetrate."[59] The capture of Narwar cut off the possibility of military assistance to Gwalior from the side of Mewar.

The target of Sikandar Lodi's ambition was Gwalior's Raja Man Singh. He belonged to an illustrious and cultured family. His great grandfather was Raja Dungar Singh. Dungar Singh's reign has become notable for two achievements: firstly, for the

57 Niamatullah, fol. 60 a-b; Abdullah, p. 68; Farishtah, I, p. 183; Nizamuddin, I, p. 324.

58 Niamatullah, fol. 61 a; Nizamuddin, I, p. 326.

59 A.N., II, pp. 342-43.

Jain sculptures on the Gwalior Rock and secondly, for his present of certain musical works to Sultan Zain-ul-Abidin of Kashmir.[60] His great grandson, Raja Man Singh (1486-1517), was the greatest ruler of the house. He was a veritable genius. He was great in war and still greater in peace. It was because of his popularity and friendship with all — Hindus and Muslims — that no Muslim ruler could gain ascendancy over him.[61] Raja Man Singh and his queen are said to have been proficient composers and singers. It is said that the Raja called a conference of musicians to make a proper classification of Ragas. Undoubtedly he was the founder of the Gwalior school of classical music.[62] He is said to have revived the Dhrupad style which had been neglected and therefore forgotten since the days of Amir Khusrau.[63] He was the author of a treatise on music entitled *Māna-kutūhala*.[64] He also got the *Rāgadarpaṇa*, a treatise on Indian classical music, translated into Persian. It is, therefore, not surprising that the famous Mughal musician Tansen originally belonged to Gwalior. The magnificent fort of Gwalior owes much of its beauty and grandeur to Raja Man Singh. He "enriched Gwalior with the great palace which crowns the eastern face of the rock,"[65] and stands as a landmark of the city.

In short, Gwalior under the Tomar Rajputs was a highly developed culture state. The Lodi sultans and the invader Babur after persistent exertion for thirty years managed to destroy it. Once its Rajas were gone, [66] it was incorporated in the Mughal

60 Nizamuddin, III, pp. 659-60; Mohibbul Hasan, *Kashmir under the Sultans*, p. 73.

61 Niamatullah, fol. 78 b.

62 V.N. Bhatkhande, *A Short Historical Survey of the Music of Upper India*, p. 18.

63 *Islamic Culture*, Vol. XXIX, 1955, p. 20.

64 *Ain.*, I, p. 681; Harihar Niwas Dwivedi, *Māna Singha aur Māna-kutūhala* (Hindi), pp. 41, 43.

65 Wolseley Haig in C.H.I., III, p. 534.

66 In the Battle of Haldighati, Raja Ram Sah, the exiled prince of Gwalior, with his son Khanderao and three hundred and fifty of his brave Tomar clan, paid the debt of gratitude with their lives. "Since the expulsion by Babur they had found sanctuary in Mewar, whose princes diminished their feeble revenue to maintain inviolate the rites of hospitality" (Wloseley Haig in C.H.I., IV, p. 116).

empire. But the people remained sullen and organised resistance to foreign rule in their own way. In the medieval period, indeed right up to the early years of the twentieth century, "the area between the Jumna and Chambal presents, for the most part, a scene of wild desolation which can hardly be equalled in the plains of India".[67] The restless oustees of Gwalior retired to the jungles and ravines on both sides of the river Chambal. From this rugged region they struck at their new rulers. They did not let the Mughals rest in peace. There are frequent references to the terror they inspired in the region of Etawah (Hatkant) and Dholpur to the north and Gwalior and Narwar to the south of Chambal during the Mughal rule. Abul Fazl writes about them: "The inhabitants of the hamlets of the town of Saket (in Etah district), which is about thirty *kos* from Agra, had not their equals for refractoriness and ingratitude. Especially eight villages of the *pargana*, which were known by the name of Athgarha were for insolence, robbery, manslaughter, boldness and turbulence such that the eye of the world had not seen their like, for they were both ruffians (or residents of inaccessible places) and occupiers of rough places, and they lived by audacity which the ignorant call manliness."[68] Akbar himself got a taste of their audacity and manliness in an encounter with them.[69] Henry Beveridge, the translator of the *Akbar Nama* says in a footnote that "it (the region) was notorious for its robbers down to our own times (end of the nineteenth century)."

This region of which Chambal ravines, Bhind and Morena have become household words was infested with decoits till very recent times and the local people, well aware of their history through stories and legends, considered them brave and gallant. Chambal ravines remained infested with anti-government elements all through. These people were freedom fighters against Muslim invaders and rulers in the medieval period and, like the

---

67 *Imp. Gaz.*, United Provinces of Agrà and Oudh, I, p. 452.

68 A.N., II, pp. 251-52; for pun on ruffians and residents of inaccessible places, see n. 4.

69 Ibid., pp. 252-255.

Bhils of Chittor, did not give up their tenor of life even after India had gained independence in 1947. Raja Man Singh Tomar was the greatest king of the region in the medieval period; Man Singh, the decoit, was the greatest bandit in our own times. Muslim invaders and rulers had turned these civilized peace-loving people into highway robbers, or guerrilla warriors as they were prone to look at themselves. It is significant that the local people even now hail as *baghis* (rebels) the outlaws whom outsiders call decoits.

All Muslim chroniclers reiterate that highway robbery was one of the methods of resistance by those who were forced to flee from civilized life into the wilds. Babur writes that when he came to Agra, "All the inhabitants had run away in terror. Neither grain for ourselves nor corn for our horses was to be had. The villages, out of hostility and hatred to us had taken to thieving and highway robbery: there was no moving on the roads."[70] And so was the case with regard to Dholpur and Gwalior whose reduction by Lodis had enraged its people. Babur says that while at Agra, "we had not been able to detach reinforcements...because the forts round about — Etawah, Dholpur and Bayana — had not yet surrendered".[71] Even after Dholpur and its environs were brought under some sort of control, the "Pagans" in the wilds did not cease their highway robbery. "Hindus of Etawah (District) succeeded on the whole in maintaining their independence against Musalman aggressors ..."[72] Akbar the Great Mughal took vigorous measures for the repression of robber tribes in Mainpuri. But he failed to incorporate Etawah.[73] Refaqat Ali Khan writes that "Akbar's matrimonial alliances indicate the extent of influence in a particular region. The absence of such alliances with Orcha, Bandugarh, Bundi, Mewar and the kingdoms of Himachal and Kumaon indicates that Akbar's control over them was not effective."[74]

70 *Babur Nama*, II, p. 524.

71 Ibid., p. 529, also, pp. 539, 540.

72 *Imp. Gaz.*, United Provinces of Agra and Oudh. I, p. 453. Muslim harassment had made them bitter and sullen. Naturally they were loyal to the British during 'the Mutiny' (Ibid., p. 455).

73 Ibid., I, pp. 439, 456; II, pp. 468-69.

74 Refaqat Ali Khan, *The Kachhwahas under Akbar and Jahangir*, p. 210.

To resume. The refugees in the forests did not only organize forays on the highways, they also harassed important Muslims in distress passing through their area. For example, after the debacle in the Battle of Kanauj (1540 CE) against Sher Shah, Humayun returned to Agra with his brothers Hindal and Askari and the ladies of the harem. On the way when he reached Bhongaon (transcribed as Bhyngang by Stewart),[75] the "villagers who were in the habit of plundering a defeated army", blockaded the road, wounded Mirza Yadgar and captured some ladies of royalty and nobility. Hindal rescued the women with great difficulty and sent them on towards Agra. These attackers were not uncivilized rustics (*ganwars*) as Gulbadan Begum is disposed to call them,[76] but guerrilla warriors who did not fail to avail of any opportunity to wreak vengeance on their tormentors. As I.H. Siddiqi rightly says, "The mass rising of the villagers and townfolk, denounced by the Mughal writers as *gaṅwars* (rustics), against the fugitive Mughals after the battle of Qanauj (1540 A.D.), cannot be rejected as their love for plunder."[77]

It is not surprising therefore that Sher Shah laid great emphasis on the security of the highways from the very beginning of his reign. By his time the population of the refugees seems to have risen very high and so also acceleration in their guerrilla activity in the form of forays on the highways near their forest habitats. Sher Shah, before he became king, had a taste of their plundering raids. For instance, Bharat Rai, the powerful Cheru Zamindar of Palamau in Bihar, gave him much trouble. The Cherus are mentioned by Abul Fazl as the principal Zamindars in Ramgarh, Chai Champa and Pundag in Palamau.[78] Bharat Rai built the fort of Deogan, one of the three strongest forts of Palamau, the two others being Kothi and Kunda. "Whenever

---

75 Jouhar, *Private Memoirs of Humayun*, English trs of *Tazkirat-ul-Waqiat* by Charles Stewart, 1832, Delhi Reprint, 1972, p. 23.

76 *The History of Humayun*, English trs of Gulbadam Begum's *Humayun Nama* by A.S. Beveridge (1901), Delhi Reprint 1972, p. 143; Persian text, p. 37.

77 Siddiqi, *Some Aspects of Afghan Despotism in India*, p. 90.

78 *Ain.*, II, p. 154n.

Sher Khan was in any trouble," Bharat Rai "used to descend from his hills and jungles and harass the tenants around Bihar, and taking to highway robbery closed the road to travellers proceeding to Gaur and Bengal, and took every opportunity of plundering horses, camels and bullocks from the camp of Sher Khan."[79] This "renowned border chieftain" appears to have harassed Sher Khan "to some purpose and to have been regarded by him as an opponent whom it was absolutely necessary to crush".[80] In about 1539-40 CE, Sher Khan sent Khawas Khan against him with orders to cut down his jungle fortress and to capture him. The officers of Sher Khan also collected revenue of both the autumn and spring harvests of these parts.[81] But these Cheru Zamindars used to retaliate and stood defiant against Muslim rule throughout.[82]

In the Chambal region, the rebellious Zamindars were ever active as vouched by the statement of Abul Fazl cited above. After ascending the throne Sher Shah brought 12,000 horsemen from Sarhind *sarkar,* and quartered them in the *pargana* of Hathkant to keep the neighbourhood under effective control, and they repressed the agriculturists of those parts. "In the fort of Gwalior, Sher Shah kept a force to which were attached 1000 matchlockmen."[83] For the protection of the roads from highway robbers he held headmen of the villages responsible to effect the surrender of those who committed crimes in their villages or who took refuge in them. If the *muqaddams* produced the offenders, the latter were punished "with the penalties laid down in the holy law". But if the *muqaddams* of the village where a murder had occurred could not produce the culprit, they themselves were put

79 Dorn, *Makhzan-i-Afghana*, p. 116.

80 Hodivala, p. 454.

81 Abbas Sarwani, *Tarikh-i-Sher Shahi*, E.D., IV, p. 368.

82 Under the mighty Mughals, Partab, the son of Balbhadra Cheru, in the time of Shahjahan was, after two invasions, compelled to pay tribute to the Mughal emperor in 1642-43. Seventeen years afterwards the country was finally conquered and annexed to the Empire by Aurangzeb in 1660 CE (Hodivala, p. 454).

83 Abbas Sarwani, op.cit., pp. 368-69; 416-17.

to death. "Under these circumstances," observes Henry Elliot, "there was of course no difficulty in getting the culprit, or at least a culprit, who was forthwith executed."[84]

In short, Sher Shah directed his governors and *amils* to see to the safety of roads and compel the people to treat merchants and travellers well. And in this he succeeded fairly well. Both the Afghan chronicler Abbas Khan and the Mughal chronicler Badaoni assert, though in hyperbolic language, that "a decrepit old woman might place a basket full of gold ornaments on her head and go on a journey, and no thief or robber would come near her, for fear of punishments which Sher Shah inflicted".[85]

The Turks and the Mughals considered the Afghans to be boorish and barbarous.[86] But in expending money on government and administration, on construction of buildings, and on works of piety, the Afghans were inferior neither to the Turks nor to the Mughals. The reforms and regulations of the Afghans, in particular of Sher Shah, were modelled on those of Sultan Alauddin Khalji. The Afghan army looked magnificent and awe-inspiring. Sher Shah built four trunk roads and 1700 *sarais*. All the Lodi and Sur sultans undertook works of piety with devotion and zeal. Sikandar Lodi founded *masjids* through out his dominions, and appointed a preacher, a reader, and a sweeper to each. He spared no pains to educate the Afghan chiefs and clansmen.[87] Sher Shah instituted an inquiry about deserving ulema, saints and saiyyads, and gave them back all the *imlak*, that is, land-grants and stipends which they had received from their predecessors. "It was the custom of the Afghans during the time of Sultans Bahlol and Sikandar...that if any Afghan received a sum of money or dress of honour (once), he received it every year... To every pious Afghan who came into his presence from Afghanistan, Sher Shah used to give money to an amount exceeding his expectations, and he would say, 'This is your share of the kingdom of

84 Ibid., p. 420 and n. on p. 421.
85 Ibid., p. 433; Badaoni, I, p. 473.
86 Abdullah, p. 11; Nizamuddin, I, p. 299; Farishtah, I, 179.
87 Nizamuddin, I, p. 336.

Hind, which has fallen into my hands, this is assigned to you, come every year to receive it.'"[88] This generosity was provided by the peasants' labours. Sher Shah took various steps to improve their condition and at the same time replenish the coffers of the state. In war or peace he did not plunder the peasants, nor destroy their cultivation, "For," said he, "if I oppress them they will abandon their villages, and the country will be ruined and deserted."[89]

Nevertheless, evidence contained in Afghan chronicles confirms continuance of use of military force in collection of revenue and flight of peasants and Zamindars into the forests. Ahmad Khan Jalwani, the *muqta* of the *sarkar* of Bayana under Bahlul and Sikandar, is reported to have used military force in collection of revenue. Finding their power of opposition inadequate, the Zamindars often decided to leave for the forests with "all the villagers".[90] Similarly, Farid Sur (later Sher Khan and Sher Shah) destroyed a number of *muqaddams* and their followers. Sher Shah "has been unnecessarily credited with the establishment of a new administrative system". What he and his son Islam Shah actually did was to continue the Lodi system, who in their turn had adopted the Khalji and Tughlaq system.[91] Sher Shah no doubt carried out many reforms. One of these, that is, "be lenient at the time of assessment but show no mercy at the time of collection", speaks for itself. He was also keen to send his "good old loyal experienced servants (or nobles belonging to his tribe) to districts which yielded good profits" and "advantages" and after two years or so transferred them and sent "other servants like them" so that they "may also prosper".[92] "This pernicious practice encouraged officials to make all that they could in the short time during which they held office."[93] It was of

88 Abbas Sarwani, op.cit., p. 424.

89 Ibid., p. 424.

90 Rizqullah, fol. 68a.

91 Siddiqi, *Afghan Despotism*, pp. 79, 146; Moreland, *Agrarian System*, pp. 76-77.

92 Abbas Sarwani, op.cit., p. 414.

93 Wolseley Haig in C.H.I., IV, p. 56.

course the Zamindars and peasants who provided these profits and advantages. Many fled into the jungles to avoid obliging his Afghan tribesmen.

Under the Mughals

The Mughal empire was the greatest empire in the contemporary world. It is famous for the intemperate epicurism of its ruling class and the redundant expenses on government institutions. This placed a heavy burden on the agriculturists who provided for their maintenance. Besides, the basic policy of impoverishing the people for political ends, enunciated in the Sultanate period, was never given up throughout the medieval period. The result was continual flight of the oppressed peasantry into the wilds during the Mughal period also. Since we have already dealt with this subject in detail elsewhere,[94] a bare summary of the situation needs to be repeated here. Under the Turks and the Afghans, the condition of the peasantry was pitiable. Except during the reigns of Firoz Shah Tughlaq and Sher Shah Sur, no serious effort was made to ameliorate their condition. Firoz Tughlaq was kind towards the peasants because he had ascended the throne at the mellowed age of forty-five and had seen their wretched plight under his predecessor Muhammad Tughlaq. Sher Shah was also considerate to the cultivators because he too had ascended to power when he was about fifty-five and possessed, knowledge about their problems from his early years.

During the Mughal period the condition of the agriculturists turned miserable; if there was any progress it was in the enhancement of taxation. According to W.H. Moreland who has made a special study of the agrarian system of Mughal India, the basic object of the Mughal administration was to obtain the revenue on an ever-ascending scale. The share that could be taken out of the peasant's produce without destroying his chances of survival was probably a matter of common knowledge in each locality. In Akbar's time, in Kashmir, the state demand was one-third, but in

94 Lal, *The Legacy of Muslim Rule in India*, p. 245-300.

reality it came to two-thirds.[95] The Jagirdars in Thatta (Sindh) did not take more than half. In Gujarat, according to Geleynsen who wrote in 1629 CE, the peasant was made to part with three-quarters of his harvest. Similar is the testimony of De Laet, Fryer and Van Twist.[96] During Akbar's reign, says Abul Fazl, evil hearted officers because of sheer greed used to proceed to villages and *mahals* and sack them.[97]

Akbar carried out many reforms; he almost reorganised the agrarian administration. But it appears that every reform meant additional burden on the tillers of the soil. Todar Mal's revenue was enhanced by successive governors of Bengal. His revenue rate in 1582 CE was as high as four times that of 1901.[98] This claim of the British administration has to be kept in mind when the greatness of the "Great Mogul" is evaluated. Conditions became intolerable by the time of Jahangir and Shahjahan when, according to Manucci, peasants were compelled to sell their women and children to meet the revenue demand.[99] Manrique writes that the peasants were "carried off.... to various markets and fairs, (to be sold) with their poor unhappy wives behind them carrying their small children all crying and lamenting ...."[100] Bernier too affirms that the unfortunate peasants who were incapable of discharging the demands of their rapacious lords, were bereft of their children, who were carried away as slaves.[101] Here was also confirmation, if not actually the beginning, of the practice of bonded labour in India.

This process of flight of peasants seems to have continued throughout the Mughal period, both in the North and the South. Writing of the days of Shahjahan, Bernier says that "many of the peasantry, driven to despair by so excerable a tyranny, abandon the country and sometimes fly to the territories of a Raja because they

95 Moreland, *From Akbar to Aurangzeb*, pp. 253-55.
96 Moreland in *Journal of Indian History*, IV, pp. 78-79 and XIV, p. 64.
97 A.N., II, pp. 159-60.
98 *Imp. Gaz.*, Bengal, I, pp. 122-23; II, p. 99.
99 Manucci, II, p. 451.
100 Manrique, II, p. 272.
101 Bernier, p. 205.

find less oppression and are allowed a greater degree of comfort".[102]

Commenting on the observation of Bernier, Satya Prakash Gupta writes that the French Doctor "said that the peasants were more lightly assessed in the territories controlled by the Rajas and in consequence fled to them to escape from the oppression of the Mughal governors. But these would not seem to be applicable to Eastern Rajasthan (Amber-Jaipur), where any deviations from the standard Mughal system are hard to discern."[103] Gupta's revenue figures for the region also bear out his statement.[104] Refaqat Ali Khan also arrives at the same conclusion. Writing about Raja Man Singh of Amber (1562-1614 CE), he writes that "He (the Raja) was very generous to his soldiers and servants but was very cruel and inhuman to his amils,"[105] tax assessors and collectors. Bernier does not specifically write about migration of peasants to any particular Raja's state, certainly not to Amber which was allied to the Mughal government as perhaps no other kingdom was. He talks in general terms about group-migration of peasants to the territories of Rajas where they found less oppression, more protection and greater degree of religious tolerance. They went to those Rajas and Zamindars who were in many ways greater than those grand lords of the Mughals of whom both Badaoni and Bernier did not fail to take notice and make mention.[106] They may have even covered long distances to reach their new masters for protection. We know that thousands of Barwaris went all the way from Gujarat to Delhi in 1320 in response to the call of their patron.

As pointed out earlier, medieval Indian society, both urban and agrarian, was to some extent an armed society. In cities and

102 Ibid., p. 226.

103 *The Agrarian System of Eastern Rajasthan*, p. 155.

104 Ibid., pp. 144-154.

105 *The Kachhwahas under Akbar and Jahangir*, p. 129, citing Farid Bhakkari, *Zakhirat-ul-Khawanin*, Karachi, 1961, I, pp. 103-111.

106 "The Hindus...are indispensables; to them belongs half the army and half the land. Neither the Hindustanis nor the Moghuls can point to such grand lords as the Hindus have among themselves" (Badaoni, II, p. 339; *Ain*, I, p. 214; Bernier, p. 40).

towns the elite carried swords like walking sticks. In villages few men were without at least a spear or bow and arrows, and they knew how to repay the insults of tax collectors. In 1632, Peter Mundy actually saw in the present-day Kanpur district, "labourers with their guns, swords and bucklers lying by them while they ploughed the ground".[107] Similarly, Manucci described how in Akbar's days the villagers of the Mathura region defended themselves against Mughal revenue-collecting officers: "The women stood behind their husbands with spears and arrows; when the husband had shot off his matchlock, his wife handed him the lance, while she reloaded the matchlock."[108] The countryside was studded with little forts, some surrounded by nothing more than mud walls but which nevertheless provided centres of the general tradition of rebellion and agrarian unrest. Armed peasants provided contingents to the Baheliyas, the Bhadauriyas, the Bachgotis, the Mandahars and the Tomars in the earlier period, to the Jats, the Marathas and the Sikhs in the later.

However, the success of such scattered resistance was limited. In spite of their growing effeminacy, there was enough of the Mughal blood in Aurangzeb's courtiers to make them delight in heartless exploitation of the hapless peasant. The downtrodden peasantry could never give serious trouble to the Mughals, except by fleeing the fields and ruining agriculture. Sir Henry Elliot aptly quotes from Ibn Khaldun, the most philosophic of all the Arabian writers upon history and social economy, to show the effect of these exactions upon the government and the people: "With the progress of luxury the wants of government and its servants increased and their zeal diminished; so that it became requisite to employ more people, and to give them higher pay. Consequently, the taxes were gradually increased, till the proprietors and working classes were unable to pay them..."[109]

An important order in the reign of Aurangzeb describes the

107 Mundy, *Travels*, II, p. 90.
108 Manucci, I, p. 134.
109 E.D., I, Appendix, pp. 477-78.

Jagirdars as demanding in theory only half but in practice actually more than the total yield.[110] Describing the conditions of Mughal empire in the later part of the seventeenth century, Dr. Tara Chand writes: "The desire of the State was to extract the economic rent, so that nothing but bare subsistence remained for the peasant." Aurangzeb's instructions were that "there shall be left for every-one who cultivates his land as much as he requires for his own support till the next crop be reaped and that of his family and for seed. This much shall be left to him, what remains is land tax, and shall go to the public treasury."[111]

This resulted in passive resistance through flight into forests and open resistance through guerrilla attacks on highways. Sher Shah had succeeded to some extent in safeguarding the interests of caravans and individuals during their journey, but soon the situation reverted back to old ways so that Jahangir was "compelled to observe, with whatever regret, that notwithstanding the frequent and sanguinary executions, the number of the turbulent and disaffected never seems to diminish".[112] William Hawkins who was in India in Jahangir's reign confirms this statement by saying that "almost a man cannot stir out of doors throughout all his dominions without great forces, for they are all become rebels".[113] They fled into forests from their fields and villages. The descendants of many of them can still be seen from Manipur to Chota Nagpur besides other regions, often in tribal dresses, carrying choppers or long bows. The tribal chiefs dwelling in almost all forests of India were a perpetual source of danger to the sultans and their governors. Far from remaining mild Hindus of the plains, they became determined fighters, urged to fury by a keen sense of honour and pride of faith.

Negative Aspects of Flight into the Wilds

The resistance of the people and their flight into the forests

110 Moreland, *From Akbar to Aurangzeb*, p. 255.
111 Tara Chand, *History of Freedom Movement in India*, I, p. 121.
112 Price, *Tarikh-i-Salim Shahi*, trs. pp. 225-26.
113 Foster, *Early Travels*, pp. 113, 114. Also Tavernier, I, p. 38.

helped them preserve their religion and independence. But in the process they and the country lost much. Life in the wilds was hard. There was not enough food, and many times the fugitives had to live only on tree roots and wild fruits. Sometimes the leaders among them resorted to highway robbery to replenish their meagre resources, but the poor among them could not have benefited much from it. Besides, brigandage in itself was a temporary expedient, insufficient to satisfy their needs properly and permanently. On the other hand, these refugees got cut off from whatever education and culture was available in the settled life in town and country. Their health also suffered because of malarial climate and debilitating diseases generally prevalent in thick forests. No medical facility was available there although sometime they treated themselves with herbal plants, roots and leaves of trees they alone could identify. But the recipe was uncertain and recovery unsure. The benefits of urbanization developing at a fast pace in the medieval period were denied to them. Their social status also declined. Their isolation in the wilds snapped their links with old associates. It resulted in their developing different rites and ceremonies, different symbols and prayers, different Gods and Goddesses from the ones they worshipped in the plains. And although they all remained Hindu, they became poor and still more poor in their isolation.

It is not the fugitives alone who suffered. The people in the inhabited plains also lost much by the retreat of their fellow-workers into the wilds. There was no ethnic or racial difference between them and their fellow beings in the plains, no difference between their hopes and aspirations. But their flight into the forests greatly reduced the combat potential of the Hindus in the countryside, resulting in unrestrained oppression by the Muslim ruling class. For example, Narwar was a great city in its heyday, next only to Gwalior in the magnificence of its temples and other edifices. It was surrounded by thick forests in which emperor Akbar used to hunt for elephants,[114] and to which people used to

114 A.N., II, p. 342.

flee during emergencies. Sikandar Lodi had attacked Narwar and remained there for full six months during which he broke temples and effectually removed every edifice of importance. Similarly, old Chanderi is in ruins, today's Chanderi is new. Had the agriculturists not moved into the jungles due to oppressive revenue demands under Shahjahan and Aurangzeb, the extensive iconoclasm of these emperors might not have been possible on such a large scale. The freedom fighters of medieval India would have helped save thousands of religious edifices from destruction, including the magnificent temples of Varanasi and Mathura, but their flight into forests left the field free for Mughal vandalism.

V
Direct Confrontation by Low Castes

Barwaris capture Delhi

Escape into the jungles to get away to safety from the tyranny of oppressive taxation was common; it formed an indirect method of resistance. There were also occasions of direct confrontation between low caste Hindus and the Muslim regime. The case of the Barwaris of Gujarat is perhaps the first case of the kind.

The leader of the Barwari insurrection in Delhi was a Hindu convert, Hasan. He was captured while only a child in the invasion of Malwa by Ain-ul-Mulk Multani in 1305 CE. He was brought to Delhi and enrolled among the personal slave boys of Sultan Alauddin Khalji. When Alauddin's son Qutbuddin Mubarak Khalji succeeded to the throne (20 April, 1320), he became highly enamoured of the youthful Hasan and made him his Wazir. He conferred upon him the title of Khusrau Khan together with all the jagirs and extraordinary distinctions which, Alauddin had bestowed on his own favourite Wazir, Malik Kafur. And he proved to be as good or bad a protege to his patron Qutbuddin as Malik Kafur had proved to Alauddin Khalji.

Intrigues in Muslim court and palace were of common occurrence, but Hindus, or at least low class Hindus, had little to do with them. These were the pursuits of politically ambitious Muslim nobles. During the Khalji and Tughlaq regimes, dozens of such rebellions had taken place, but one such insurrection goes to the credit of Hindu low caste Barwaris.

There were reasons for Hasan to kill his patron and for the Barwaris to wreak vengeance against the Muslims. Some eunuch slaves could not forget the circumstance of their conversion. Some others resented their low status vis-a-vis their foreign counterparts. The humiliation caused by the infliction of unnatural carnal acts of their masters made some others sullen and revengeful. Khusrau Khan, it appears, was such an one. Outwardly he surrendered his body to the Sultan, but actually he hated the latter and thirsted for his blood.[1] He collected his Barwari clansmen in Delhi in strength, got Qutbuddin killed (September 1320) with their help, and ascended the throne as Sultan Nasiruddin Khusrau Shah.

Khusrau Shah was the leader. It was actually the Barwaris who rose in revolt. There is difference of opinion about who the Barwaris were and how low was their tribe.[2] But all chroniclers including Barani, Amir Khusrau and Ibn Battuta credit them with low social status coupled with bravery and readiness to lay down their lives for their masters. The Barwaris had heard or eye-witnessed the atrocities of the Muslim soldiers in Gujarat during its invasion in 1299 CE. The massacres in Anhilwara, Asavalli (near Ahmedabad), Cambay, Vanmanthali, Surat etc. had earned Alauddin, according to the *Rasmala*, the nickname of *Khuni* (shedder of blood). A number of monasteries, temples and palaces in Gujarat had been destroyed.[3] So, when a call came from their clansman Khusrau, thousands of Barwaris trudged hundreds of miles on foot and carts for the capital of Hindustan to avenge the sack of Gujarat. According to Farishtah, there were forty thousand Barwaris in Delhi at the time of their of insurrection.[4]

They helped in planning and executing the assassination of Qutbuddin. Thereafter they finished all the scions of the Khalji house, all the possible claimants to the throne. Khusrau Shah ascended the throne; he usurped the chief wife of Qutbuddin and other Barwaris took possession of Muslim girls. Copies of the Quran were torn to pieces and used for seats for idols which were placed in the niches (*mehrabs*) of the mosques.[5] Idol worship began to be practised inside the royal palace. Khusrau Shah,

---

1 Barani, pp. 391-92.
2 For details Lal, *Khaljis*, pp. 309-12.
3 Barani, pp. 251-52; Isami, *Futuh-us-Salatin*, Persian text, p. 243; *Indian Antiquary*, 1897, p. 187.
4 Farishtah, I, p. 127.
5 Barani, p. 411.

writes Ibn Battuta, "forbade the slaughter of cows according to the custom of infidel Hindus... (because) they hold the cow in great esteem".[6] A latter-day chronicler, Nizamuddin Ahmad, says that mosques were also destroyed.[7] According to the contemporary chronicler Barani, infidelity gained ascendancy and the Musalmans were subjected to humiliations unprecedented in the history of the Sultanate. Yahiya's account is not exaggerated. He says that the Hindus (i.e. Barwaris), confident of their position as relations of Sultan Nasiruddin Khusrau Shah, subjected the Muslims to cruelty.[8] They were in control of Delhi for a little more than four months. During this period some of the disgruntled nobles were murdered in their houses. Others were brought into the palace by means of guile and treachery and beheaded. Qazi Ziyauddin's house was raided and bestowed on Randhol, a maternal uncle of Khusrau Shah. He had played a leading role in the coup and was given the title of Raya Rayan.

The assertion of some medieval and modern writers that the Barwaris tried to establish Hindu Raj in the Sultanate is not borne out by facts. They had known Muslims breaking Hindu temples and burning their religious books. They responded with counter measures. They paid the Muslims in their own coin as it were. This was courageous enough. Beyond this there seems to have been no plan, although according to Barani, Hindus in many cities were very happy and optimistic at the rise of Khusrau.[9] Many Muslim nobles in Delhi and provincial governors also accepted Khusrau's sovereignty and fought on his behalf.

Even if the idea of establishing Hindu Raj was present in some minds, it was swiftly put to an end by the success of Ghiyasudin Tughlaq who invaded Delhi, killed Khusrau and stamped out Barwari resistance. Most of them fled towards Gujarat and many of them were put to death by Ghiyasuddin's

---

6 Ibn Battuta, p. 47.
7 Nizamuddin, I, p. 187.
8 Yahiya, p. 87.
9 Barani, p. 412.

excited soldiery on the road.[10] But the Barwari revolt forms a very significant episode in the resistance of the low caste Hindus in the early history of medieval India.

Khokhars continue Resistance

The Khokhars had tenaciously opposed the early Muslim invaders and killed Muhammad Ghauri. They continued their resistance in after years. Prior to the turbulent times of Timur's invasion, the Khokhars took Lahore in 1394 CE. They tried to gain advantage against the Delhi Sultanate by aligning with the conqueror and promising him help in his attack on Delhi.[11] But their leader, Shaikha Khokhar, hardly meant to keep his word and for this 'treachery' he was beheaded by Timur,[12] while his son, Jasrath Khokhar, was carried a prisoner to Samarqand. On Timur's death, Jasrath effected his escape[13] and returned to his homeland to resume the leadership of his tribe. During the weak rule of the Saiyyad Dynasty he established his headquarters at Talwara on the right bank of the Chenab lying about 40 kms. north-west of Jammu and 80 kms. north of Sialkot.[14] For the next forty years Jasrath and other Khokhar leaders kept up a continual resistance against Delhi sultans and the Raja of Jammu, sometimes inviting help from abroad and at others joining rebels at home against the Sultanate. Their open resistance came to an end only with the death of Jasrath in 1442 CE. But resistance of this tribe was hard to crush. For two and a half centuries they had defied the Muslim conquerors and rulers openly and thereafter indirectly. In the process many were killed, captured, converted and sold as slaves. But many more successfully retained their tribal culture and independence. Before establishing his authority

10 Ishwari Prasad, *Qaraunah Turks*, I, pp. 16-17. Also Lal, *Khaljis*, pp. 304-307, 309-312 for detailed references.

11 Haji-ud-Dabir, *Zafar-ul-Walih*, III, p. 905.

12 Yahiya, p. 157; Badaoni, I, p. 264; Nizamuddin, I, p. 251; Yazdi, *Zafar Nama*, II, pp. 142-44; Farishtah, I, 154, 159.

13 J.A.S.B., XL, 1871, Pt. I, p. 80.

14 For a detailed discussion on the Khokhar stronghold see Lal, *Twilight*, Appendix B, pp. 321-22.

in Delhi in 1451 CE, Bahlol Lodi thought it wise to patch up a peace with the Khokhars.[15]

Gonds combat Asaf Khan

The present state of the Gonds gives the impression as if they have always been a backward people. Such also is the belief created by European anthropologists, sociologists, and historians. But actually their history has a very different picture to offer.

The origins of the Gond kingdom in Central India are shrouded in obscurity. It is, however, known that it had existed for nearly ten centuries before it was invaded by the Muhammadans.[16] The Gonds were an ancient people. As their power got organised, their chiefs were assimilated with the Paramara and the Kalachuri clans of Rajputs. They had their own annalists although the latter help little in reconstructing their history.[17] It is, however, certain that the Gond rulers had gained importance by the sixteenth century. Soon after that the Gond kingdom was visited by a Muslim invasion.

Abul Fazl narrates the events leading to the attack on the Gond kingdom during the reign of Mughal emperor Akbar. "In the spacious territories of India," writes he, "there is a country called Gondwara (Gondwana), viz., the country inhabited by Gonds. The east part of the country adjoins Ratanpur which belongs to Jharkhand, and the west is contiguous to Raisen which belongs to the province of Malwa. Its length (from E to W) may be 150 *kos*. On the north is the country of Pannah, and on the south the Deccan. Its width may be 80 *kos*. The country is called Gadha-Katanga (modern Jabalpur). It is an extensive tract and is full of forts, and contains populous cities and towns, so that truthful narrators have stated that Gadha-Katanga contained

---

15 Khokhars are still found in large numbers in the Punjab. Malik Bahauddin Khokhar became the chief of Sanaur in Patiala. In 1748 he was conquered by Ala Singh who founded the Patiala State (*Imp. Gaz.*, Punjab, II, p. 309).

16 C.H.I., IV, p. 87.

17 Charles Grant, *The Gazetteer of the Central Provinces*, Introduction, pp. xiv-xv, xlix.

70,000 inhabited villages... The capital is the fortress of Chauragarh..."[18]

"Since the first appearance of Islam," comments Abul Fazl, "when great rulers conquered India, though their reigns were long, the bird of victory of none of them was able to fly to the pinnacles of those strong forts..."[19] The country was full of rain forests and therefore rather isolated. Occasionally, a Muslim army had passed through it without causing harm. For example, in 1296 CE prince Alauddin Khalji had marched through Gondwana ("by devious and unfrequented jungle tracks") to lead a campaign against Devagiri.[20] Similarly, prince Jalal Khan, the brother of Ibrahim Lodi and a rival of the latter for the throne, arrived at Garha-Katanga to seek shelter with the Gond Raja Sangram Shah (1480-1530). But not to embroil himself in the Lodi civil strife and also to gain the goodwill of the Sultan, Sangram took Jalal captive and sent him to Ibrahim at Agra.[21]

"At this time, when Asaf Khan became the jagirdar of the Sarkar of Karra, and conquered the territory of Pannah," writes Abul Fazl, "the sovereignty of that country (Garha-Katanga) had come to a woman named Durgavati, who was generally known as the Rani. She was distinguished for courage, counsel and munificence, and by virtue of these elect qualities she had brought the whole of that country under her sway." She was the only daughter of the Chandel king Kirti Singh of Kalinjar in district Banda in U.P. The Raja gave her in marriage to prince Dalpat Sah of Gondwana. On becoming the Raja, Dalpat Sah ruled for seven years and he "had many Rajputs in his cavalry and infantry", including Paramara Rajputs. After his death, Rani Durgavati in concurrence with Adhar Kayastha and Man Brahmana became regent of her five year old son, Veer Narayan. He held

18 A.N., II, pp. 323-33. For Panna, pp. 229, 280-83. See also Charles Grant, op.cit., p. 209. For a critical note on Garha-Katanga see Lal, *Twilight*, Appendix D, pp. 331-32.

19 A.N., II, pp. 323-24.

20 Farishtah, I, p. 95.

21 Nizamuddin, I, p. 348; Badaoni, I, p. 433; Farishtah, I, p. 190.

the title of Raja and his mother Durgavati exercised the real authority. "Of all the sovereigns of this dynasty," says Sir W. Sleeman, "she lives most in the recollection of the people; she carried out many highly useful works in different parts of her kingdom, and one of the large reservoirs near Jabalpur is still called the 'Rani Talao', in memory of her. During the fifteen years of her regency she did much for the country, and won the hearts of the people, while her end was as noble and devoted as her life had been useful."[22] Her abilities were manifest both in work of peace and art of war. She had great contests with Baz Bahadur of Malwa and the Miana Afghans between 1555 and 1560 and was always victorious.[23] "She had 20,000 good cavalry with her in her battles, and one thousand famous elephants... She was a good shot with gun and arrow, continually went out a-hunting, and shot with precision animals of the chase. It was her custom that whenever she heard that a tiger had made his appearance she did not drink water till she had shot him."[24]

In tiger-shooting, possession of wealth, and acts of bravery she can be compared with Nur Jahan Begum, the queen of emperor Jahangir.[25] In his memoirs Jahangir gloats over the achievements of Nur Jahan in tiger-hunting. The description of Abul Fazl of the brave deeds of Durgavati in tiger-shooting is equally appreciative if not more. Nor were the wealth and art treasures possessed by Durgavati inferior to those of Nur Jahan.[26] When the Gond fort of Chauragarh surrendered "there fell into the hands of Asaf Khan, and his men an incalculable amount of gold and silver. There were coined and uncoined gold, decorated utensils, jewels, pearls, figures, pictures, jewelled and decorated idols, figures of animals made wholly of gold and other rarities."[27]

---

22 Cited by Charles Grant, *op. cit.*, p. 283.

23 Farishtah, I, p. 254; II, pp. 273-74.

24 A.N., II, pp. 326-327.

25 *Tuzuk-i-Jahangiri*, I, p. 375; II, pp. 104-105.

26 For Nur Jahan's wealth see Lal, *The Mughal Harem*, pp. 72-74.

27 A.N., II, p. 332. For the prosperity of the Gond Kingdom see Charles Grant, op. cit., Introduction, pp. xxxiii-iv and Col. Sleeman's note on Rani Durgavati, loc.cit.

The coin was said to include a hundred large pots full of gold *ashrafis* of Alauddin Khalji. According to Vincent Smith, "It is surprising that the ruler of a country so wild as Gondwana, or Garha-Katanga as the Persian authors call it, should have accumulated such a rich treasure."[28] It is not that surprising, though. It is customary with Persian and later European writers to belittle the achievements of 'aboriginal' and 'tribal' kingdoms and consider them half-civilized if not outright savages. But these people had their own culture, their own civilization, as shown in the case of Gondwana and the example of its Rani Durgavati. Fortunately, Abul Fazl's rather rare notice in the *Akbar Nama* has resurrected her from oblivion. He focuses on her great qualities as a wife, as a mother, as a queen, as an administrator and as a warrior. At least in his praise of Durgavati he cannot be accused of exaggeration because he was writing about an enemy of his model Shahinshah.

It was the wealth of the Gondwana queen[29] that whetted the thirst of Khawaja Abdul Majid Asaf Khan Harvi to lead a campaign against Garha-Katanga in 1564.[30] Emperor Akbar ordered him to attack the kingdom with 10,000 cavalry and abundant infantry under some famous commanders and a large number of holders of fiefs in that quarter. There was no justification, no reason for Akbar to invade Gondwana and annex it to the Mughal empire except the spirit of aggression born of superiority in military strength. Vincent Smith's statement in this regard is worth quoting: "Akbar's attack on a princess of a character so noble was mere aggression, wholly unprovoked and devoid of all justification other than the lust for conquest and plunder." He is joined by Wolseley Haig who cites one of the Happy Sayings of Akbar that "a monarch should be ever intent on conquest, otherwise

28 Smith, *Akbar the Great Mogul*, pp. 51-52.

29 A.N., II, p. 327.

30 Asaf Khan was a title. There were three Asaf Khans in Akbar's reign. The famous elder brother of Nur Jahan and father of Mumtaz Mahal was the fourth Asaf Khan. Vincent Smith rightly points out that later in Akbar's reign two other nobles successively received the title of Asaf Khan and therefore the conqueror of Gondwana is conveniently distinguished as Asaf Khan I. Farishtah (I, p. 254) calls him Asaf Khan Harvi.

his neighbours rise in arms against him".[31]

"Suddenly the news arrived that the victorious army had reached Damoh which is one of the important cities of the country." At this her soldiers scattered in order to defend their families and not more than 500 men remained with her. In spite of this her determination to "die with glory than to live with ignominy" was unshaken. She rightly argued with her minister Adhar that "if the king (Akbar) were here in person it would have been proper for her to wait upon him. What did that fellow (Asaf Khan) know of her rank?" She entered the forest of Garha to organize defence. All her men — there were about 5,000 collected by then — set their hearts on fighting. The Rani put armour on her breast and a helmet on her head.

The battle was joined at Barha village (some ten miles from Jabalpur) and many on both sides fell to the dust. Three hundred Moguls were killed. "The Rani was victorious and pursued the fugitives, and emerged from the ravine." Asaf Khan came with his artillery and fortified the entrance to the pass. Another battle was fought. Three times the Rani's son, Raja Veer Narayan, repulsed the Mughal army but on the third occasion he was wounded. She ordered trusted men to remove him to a place of safety. On this account a great many left the field of battle so that not more than 300 men remained with her. But there was no weakening of the Rani's resolution. "An arrow from the bow of fate struck her right temple, and she courageously drew it out and flung it from her. The point remained in the wound, and would not come out. Just then another arrow struck her neck. That, too, she drew out with the hand of courage, but the excessive pain made her swoon. Then she drew her dagger, and herself inflicted the blow, and died in a virile fashion. A large number of her devoted followers fell in her service."[32] One is once again tempted to compare the martial feats of Rani Durgavati in 1564 with those of Nur Jahan against Mahabat Khan in 1626.[33] Only

31 Smith, op.cit., p. 50; C.H.I., IV, p. 88.

32 A.N., II, pp. 327-31.

33 Beni Prasad, *History of Jahangir,* pp. 354-58; Sir Richard Burn in C.H.I., IV, p. 175.

Durgavati emerges the braver.

The war continued. After two months Asaf Khan proceeded to the fort of Chauragarh where Raja Veer Narayan was convalescing. The fort of Chaurgarh was built on a high forest hill difficult to climb. It was a very safe place for men seeking shelter and wealth meant for preservation. That is why Veer Narayan had retired to it for recovery. The Raja led his forces out and died fighting bravely. A *jauhar* was performed. All the female inmates of the fort were reduced to ashes except two women — Kamalavati, the Rani's sister, and the other a daughter of Puragarha whom they had brought for marrying to the Raja but who had not yet been united to him. A large piece of timber had screened them from the flames and protected them. *"They obtained honour by being sent to kiss the threshold of the Shahinshah."* This is all that Akbar got from Gondwana because most of the treasure and elephants obtained in the campaign were retained by Asaf Khan who "sent none of those rarities or splendid jewels" to Akbar.[34] In fact, Asaf Khan made Garha his place of refuge. He recruited fresh troops and built up a strong force with the treasures seized from Gondwana and sought refuge there when he rebelled against Akbar.[35]

In short, Akbar gained little from the Gondwana campaign; he had only destroyed the kingdom and its people. There was a time when Gondwana was counted as a great kingdom inhabited by a civilized people as the history of Rani Durgavati and her son Veer Narayan shows. There was a time when it could boast of a large number of great and small Rajas and Rais. Even after the fall of Garha-Katanga and Chauragarh, there still remained the Raja of Garha, the Raja of Garola, the Raja of Harya, the Raja of Salwani, the Raja of Danaki, the Raja of Kathola, the Raja of Mugda, the Raja of Manola, the Raja of Deohar, and the Raja of Lanji.[36] The Gond rulers had their own developed civilization. They

34 A.N., II, p. 332. Also Suresh Mishra, *Garhā ke Gond Rājya kā Utthān aur Patan*, p. 59.

35 A.N., II, pp. 379, 382-83.

36 Ibid. p. 324 and footnotes.

encouraged development of architecture and patronized music.[36a] But the country and the people went down after the Mughal occupation. In Abul Fazl's own days "when by the revolutions of time the country is no longer the old regime," the Gonds "mostly live in the wilds. Having chosen this (forest wilds) as their abode, they devote themselves to eating and drinking and to venery. They are a low caste tribe and the people of India despise them and regard them as outside the pale of their realm and religion."[37] Thus the Gonds, a civilized people as per medieval standards, became a low tribe under Muslim rule and have remained so since then. For, about the end of the nineteenth century, Charles Grant wrote that "the Gonds form at present the lowest stratum of Hindu social system, allowed to take rank above none but the most despicable outcastes..."[38]

Though Asaf Khan Harvi, the general of Akbar, had raided the hilly region of Gondwana and stormed the extensive fortress of Chauragarh, the region "had never been brought under direct Mughal rule". So that even Akbar's revenue regulations did not apply to Gondwana.[39] A ruler in its neighbourhood, Jujhar Singh of Bundelkhand, looked at it with wistful eyes, attacked Chauragarh in 1634 and treacherously put to death its Gond Raja, Prem Narayan. The son of the dead Raja appealed to Shahjahan who appointed prince Aurangzeb to bring the aggressor to book. Negotiating the thick jungles surrounding Jujhar's capital Orchha, Aurangzeb attacked him. Jujhar fled and was hotly pursued by the Mughals. The Gonds look their revenge and killed Jujhar Singh and one of his sons in the jungles where they had sought refuge by hiding.[40] By the end of the century, the Marathas emerged as a dominating anti-Mughal force and the rallying point of all rebels against the Delhi empire. They were creating disturbances in Malwa, Gondwana and Bundelkhand.

36a Suresh Misra, op.cit., pp. 183-194.
37 A.N., II, p. 323.
38 Charles Grant, op. cit., Introduction, p. xiv.
39 C.H.I., IV, p. 464.
40 Sarkar, *A Short History of Aurangzeb*, pp. 10-11; C.H.I., IV, p. 195.

Gondwana remained a storm centre in Aurangzeb's reign on account of its vicinity to Malwa and Berar. Jadunath Sarkar summarizes the situation thus: "The great Gond kingdom of Garha had been dismembered and ruined by Akbar and its royal line sank into obscurity in the middle of the seventeenth century, when the predominance among the Gond people passed to the chiefs of Deogarh and Chanda. Their accumulated treasure, herds of elephants and collections of gems locally quarried, made them objects of cupidity to the Mughal government... The Deogarh royal family embraced Islam in order to retain their lands (1670)... Hindu and Muhammadan cultivators were encouraged to settle in them on equal terms with Gonds."[41] The Muslim Gond Rajas had resisted Mughal intrusion with the help of the Marathas and Chhatrasal Bundela. At the end of the medieval period the region was taken over by the Marathas.

The history of Gondwana is interesting in the extreme. While Muslim armies were marching and remarching from the North to the South, and the Hindu dynasties of the Deccan were succumbing to the invaders, the kingdom of Gondwana could be counted among independent powers in Central India. In the list of Akbar's dominions given in the *Ain-i-Akbari*, Garha is included as a division of the government of Malwa; but the Muhammadan power seems to have been faintly felt there, at any rate after Akbar's death, for the princes of Garha-Mandla carried on their affairs in almost entire independence.[42] A kingdom which struggled and survived for two hundred years, left its remnants in the Gond people everywhere in India. At the end of the nineteenth century the Gonds were to be found as far east as Bengal and Orissa,[43] in Berar and Madras in the south,[44] in Benaras[45] and the Baghelkhand region,[46] and along the Vindhya and Satpura

---

41 In C.H.I., IV, p. 314. Also Charles Grant, op. cit., pp. 143-145.
42 Charles Grant, op. cit., Introduction pp. xlviii, 225.
43 *Imp. Gaz.*, Bengal, II, p. 312.
44 *Imp. Gaz.*, Central India, p. 116.
45 *Imp. Gaz.*, United Provinces of Agra and Oudh, II, p. 123.
46 *Imp. Gaz.*, Central India, p. 409.

ranges in Central India.[47] In the erstwhile Bhopal State, in the Nizamat-i-Janab or south district, "the remains of a large palace belonging to its original Gond owners... are still standing. Two interesting Gond forts exist at Bari and Chaukigarh."[48]

Bhils support Rana Pratap against Akbar

If the Gonds directly confronted the Mughals, the Bhils fought them indirectly by joining the army of Rana Pratap against emperor Akbar. According to Abul Fazl, "the savage denizens of those wilds who in their language are called Bhils",[49] mainly resided in Central India, Malwa, Gujarat and Rajasthan in the medieval times.[50] Their principal home is the hilly country between Abu and Asirgarh in North Deccan. In Rajasthan, they are still living in a state of semi-independence in the southern part of Mewar region. "It is not easy to describe a tribe that includes every stage of civilization, from the wild hunter of the hills to the orderly and hard-working peasants of the lowlands."[51] James Todd calls them Vanputras or children of the forest. The typical Bhil is small, dark, and broad-nosed, but well-built and ugly. He is truthful and honest, but thriftless, excitable, and given to drink.[52] The Bhils are scantily dressed; the apparel of a Bhil is a dirty rag round his head and a loin cloth of limited length.

They never allow an enemy to trespass their country without inflicting serious injuries on him. A war-cry (*kilki*) from a Bhil lad would cause hundreds of them to assemble and dash forward against the enemy. Their main weapons consist of a small sword or bow and arrows. They fight on foot; they have no horses. They specialized in guerrilla warfare. Because of them the chiefs of Mewar were never short of manpower in times of emergency.[53]

---

47 Ibid., p. 91.

48 Ibid., pp. 243, 249, 259-60.

49 A.N., II, p. 354.

50 C.H.I., IV, pp. 192, 315.

51 *Imp. Gaz.*, Central India, pp. 81-82.

52 *Imp. Gaz.*, Rajputana, p. 87.

53 For a detailed note on them see *Rajputana Gazetteer,* Mewar Residency, 1908. Also J.A.S.B., XLIV, Part I, 1875, pp. 347-388.

Their needs were few. They were paid no salary. In times of war they were sometimes given food by the Ranas which was subsidied by a tax called *grasa* collected from the people.[54]

Bhils have secured a niche in history by their deeds of devotion and valour, particularly in their role in Rajasthan's history after the Battle of Haldighati. Rana Pratap of Chittor had inherited a precarious dominion from his father and an implacable enemy in the mighty Mughal emperor. Akbar's campaign of 1576 was intended to destroy the Rana utterly. "The wily Mogul arrayed against Pratap his kindred in faith as well as blood", for, as Vincent Smith puts it, Rana Pratap's "patriotism was his offence".[55] He was not prepared to accept the position of an humble vassal. He therefore began the transformation of Mewar into a union of the nobly born lords and the low-born Bhils, "the equal pillars of his power... Pratap was the first to recognize the worth of the Bhils who were in majority living in the south-western part of Mewar. The state emblem bears testimony to this day to the equal status given to the Bhil where both Pratap and Bhil are standing on either side of Eklingji, the titular deity of Mewar."[56] As has already been mentioned earlier, it was necessary for certain Rajput chiefs like those of Mewar, Dungarpur, Banswara and Chandrawat Thakurs of Malwa, to be marked on the brow with a Bhil's blood at the time of accession.[57] During Rana Pratap's travels and travails the Bhils became his devoted friends and followers. Their martial qualities — their habit of climbing the hills, jumping over the thorny bushes with ease and bearing all kinds of privations — were their special qualities.

In the Battle of Haldighati or Gogunda, in June 1576, the Rana gathered his force at the mouth of a pass at the base of a mountain. Above and below the pass were posted the Rajputs; on the cliffs and pinnacles overlooking the field of battle, stood the faithful Bhils with the bows and arrows, and large stones to roll

54 G.N. Sharma, *Mewar and the Mughal Emperors,* p. 193.
55 Smith, op. cit., pp. 106-07.
56 G.N. Sharma, op.cit., p. 86 and note 14. Also p. 84.
57 *Imp. Gaz.,* Central India, pp. 84, 219, 235.

upon the enemy.[58] The battle was fierce as attested to by all chroniclers, Persian and Rajasthani. The Rajputs belonging to various houses began to strew the field with their bodies and blood. "Scattered hordes of sanguinary, grotesque savages (so the determined blood-thirsty Bhils would have looked), pushed from the mountain side and began to make assault upon the Mughal flanks. Tribal blood poured out for the defence of the country."[59] The Mughals defied the attack of the Rajputs and Bhil arrays with obstinate determination,[60] and the Rajputs lost in the end. Rana Pratap, having been wounded, sped away mounted on his beloved steed Chetak. He was obliged to retire to remote fastnesses and remained untraceable mainly because of his faithful Bhil followers.[61] Later on Rana Pratap recovered all Mewar excepting Chittor, Ajmer and Mandalgarh. His Rajput associates and Bhil followers had taken a vow that until the time their motherland was not freed they would not eat from metal plates but only out of tree-leaves, that they would not sleep on bedsteads but only on the bare ground, and that they would renounce all comforts. The bravest among them even left Chittor for good.

The population of the Bhils in south and south-eastern Mewar is about 12 per cent of the total population of Mewar. This large percentage is there due to many reasons. The Bhils did not perform any *jauhar* of their women and children as was common with the Rajputs, and their population did not suffer decimation as did that of the Rajputs during Muslim attacks as for example in the time of Alauddin Khalji, Bahadur Shah of Gujarat, and Akbar. The gory massacres ordered by all these three invaders also did not affect the Bhil tribals. On the other hand, in emergencies like the one in 1679 CE, when Rana Raj Singh (1652-1707) was fighting the Mughals, the Bhils of Ogna, Panarwa, Jawas etc. were ordered, because of their considerable

58 Tod, *Annals and Antiquities of Rajasthan*, I, p. 270; A.N., III, p. 245.

59 G.N. Sharma, op. cit., p. 100, quoting from the Mss of *Amarakāvya Vanshāvali* and *Rāja Ratnākara.*

60 Nizamuddin, I, p. 333.

61 G.N. Sharma, op. cit., p. 110; Tod, op. cit., I, pp. 398-400.

numbers, to resist the enemy in the southern part of the country. Dr. Gopi Nath Sharma, who has made a special study of the history of Mewar, writes: "From the time of (Rana) Sanga to Raj Singh we come across a large number of fighters who belonged to various castes inhabiting the country. The names of Garibdas (Brahmin), Bhama Shah and Dayal Shah (Vaishya), Punja and Rama (Bhils) are the instances."[62] Surely, during wars all classes of people fought as bravely as any others, but the role of the Bhils and Minas was special. During such times many people of the upper castes might not have been able to preserve their old ways of life, and might have lost even their caste to drift into backward classes.

We are, however, concerned mainly with the Bhils whose deeds of valour, loyalty and perseverance have come down to our own times. The Bhils are part of the general Hindu population. Some even claim to be Rajput. Mixed Bhil and Rajput tribes are called Bhilala and Bhumiar.[63] The Bhils inhabit Vindhya and Satpura ranges. They are found in large numbers in Jaora in Central India. In Nasik, Bhils live in hamlets known as Bhilvadas.[64] Bhilwara city in Rajasthan takes its name from them. Bhils are custodians of the temple of Kala Bhairava (Shiva) in the Pachmarhi Hills of Madhya Pradesh.[65] Surely, like the Gonds, the numbers of the Bhils increased in the medieval period.

Satnamis confront Aurangzeb's Army

It has been seen earlier that in the medieval period the Chamars formed a major section of Hindu society, particularly in western Uttar Pradesh. It has also been seen that while the high

---

62 "I have seen," writes Dr. Sharma, "swords, shields, bows and arrows in some of the poorest families of Mewar preserved as relics of glory of their ancestors who must have taken daring part in one or other warlike engagements" (G.N. Sharma, op. cit., pp. 185 and n2).

63 *Imp.Gaz.*, Central India, p. 82. Also *Imp. Gaz.*, Rajasthan, p. 89.

64 *Imp. Gaz.*, Bombay Presidency, I, p. 459, also pp. 148-149; *Imp. Gaz.*, Central India, p. 299, also pp. 52, 91.

65 Charles Grant, op. cit., Introduction, p. cxxii.

caste people sometimes submitted to force or temptation of the Muslim regime, the Chamars and other low caste people were reluctant to do so. In this attitude they were as much inspired by their religious reformers as by their inherent bravery. In the seventeenth century they rose in revolt against the Mughal government. Their movement is known as the Satnami insurrection.

The *Satnami* sect was an offshoot of the Raidasis. Their stronghold in the seventeenth century was Narnaul, situated about 100 kms. south-west of Delhi. The contemporary chronicler Khafi Khan credits them with a good character. They followed the professions of agriculture and trade on a small scale. They dressed simply, like *faqirs*. They shaved their heads and so were called *mundiyas* also. They came into conflict with imperial forces. It began as a minor trouble, but developed into a war of Hindu liberation from the persecution of Aurangzeb. Soon some five thousand Satnamis were in arms. They routed the *faujdar* of Narnaul, plundered the town, demolished its mosques, and established their own administration. The uprising infected the Hindu population of Agra and Ajmer. Detachments of the imperial army were defeated, and the insurgents advanced on Delhi. A panic spread throughout the Mughal army. It was with great difficulty that Muslim soldiers could be brought to face the enemy. Confidence was restored only when Aurangzeb took personal command and sent 10,000 troops with artillery (March, 1672). Facing a most obstinate battle, two thousand Satnamis fell on the field and many more were slain during the pursuit.[66] Those who escaped spread out into small units so that today there are about 15 million Satnami Harijans found in Madhya Pradesh, Maharashtra, Bihar and Uttar Pradesh.[67]

Jats, Marathas and Sikhs fight the Mughals

Jats and Khokhars enthusiastically fought against Mahmud of Ghazni on many occasions. They kept up the tradition in later

66 Sarkar, op. cit., p. 161; C.H.I., IV, pp. 243-44.
67 Also see the last chapter.

years. The Jats in particular continued their resistance to the Mughals till the time the Mughal empire met its end. The area of their operation extended from the Salt Range mountains, through Punjab and Haryana to Mathura and Agra. Their resistance to Muslim invaders or compromise with Muslim rulers forms part of the history of the region and need not be related in detail till we reach the seventeenth century. Then their resistance gained fresh momentum.

The religious policy of Aurangzeb resulting in open attacks on Hinduism stirred the Jats into direct action. In 1661-62 CE, Abdun Nabi Khan, the *faujdar* of Mathura, built a Jama Masjid in the heart of the city on the ruins of a Hindu temple. In 1666, he forcibly removed the carved stone railing from Keshav Rai's temple. As a consequence of these and other injustices against the Hindus, the Jat peasantry rose in 1669 under the leadership of Gokla (Gokul) the Zamindar of Tilpat. Abdun Nabi marched out to attack them but was shot dead during the encounter. Flushed with victory, Gokla looted the *pargana* of Sadabad, and the disorder spread to the adjacent district of Agra.

Aurangzeb sent strong forces under high officers to stamp out the rebellion. The insurgents who mustered 20,000 strong, mostly Jat and other stalwart peasants, encountered the imperial forces at a place 32 kilometres from Tilpat. But after a long and bloody contest the Jats gave way before the superior discipline and artillery of the Mughals. The contest was indeed terrible. On the victor's side 4,000 men fell and on the Jat's 5,000. Seven thousand persons including Gokla and his family were taken prisoner. "The Jat leader's limbs were hacked off one by one on the platform of the police office of Agra, and his family was forcibly converted to Islam."[68] Peace was restored to the Agra district, but only for a time. In 1686, the second Jat rising began under the leadership of Raja Ram. Meanwhile in 1675, the Sikh Guru Tegh Bahadur had been beheaded by the orders of Aurangzeb. His son, Govind Singh, the tenth and the last of the

68 Sarkar, op. cit., p. 161.

Gurus, was not the man to leave his father's death unavenged. He organised the sect into an implacable enemy of the Mughal empire. Most of his recruits (Sikh converts) were Jats, "the best raw materials for soldiers under proper training and leadership".[69]

The endless wars in which Aurangzeb became involved in the Deccan in 1681 and which were to continue till his death, provided the Jats welcome opportunities to harass the Mughals in the North. Long caravans of merchandise, State revenue and army provisions, so frequently making their way to the royal court under slender escort, passed directly through the Jat country from Delhi and Agra to Dholpur and thence through Malwa to the Deccan. These provided great temptation to the Jats and other Hindu tribes. In 1685, two Jats leaders, Raja Ram and Ram Chehra, petty zamindars of Sinsani and Sogar, assumed leadership of the Jats. They trained their clansmen in group organization and open warfare. They built *garhis* (small forts) amidst their almost trackless jungles and strengthened them with mud walls that could defy artillery. Every Jat peasant was given practice in wielding the staff and the sword. They began to raid the king's highway and carried their depredetions up to the suburbs of Agra. They closed other highways to traffic, and plundered whatever they could lay their hands on. They killed the Mughal warrior Aghar Khan and in 1688 they attacked Mahabat Khan, then marching to his viceroyalty of the Punjab. Shortly afterwards, they plundered Akbar's tomb at Sikandara.

In 1688, Raja Ram was killed in an intra-clan war of the Rajputs. The Mughals mounted a campaign against the Jats and laid siege to Sinsani. But the campaign in the jungles of the Jat country severely taxed the invading army. The fort could be stormed only in January 1690. After three hours of fighting the Jats lost 1500 men. On the imperial side, 200 Mughals and 700 Rajputs were slain or wounded. The other Jat stronghold of Sogar was also surprised. The new Jat leader Churaman, a nephew of Raja Ram, went into hiding in "nooks and corners" of

69 C.H.I., IV, pp. 245-46.

jungles unknown to the imperialists. He increased the number of his soldiers, enrolled musketeers, raised a troop of cavalry, and "having robbed many of the ministers of the court on the road, he attacked the royal wardrobe and the revenue sent from the provinces".[70] This was nothing new. The route between the North and the South was never safe for the royalists ever since Muslim armies had marched into the Deccan and stirred the people to resistance. During the reign of Muhammad bin Tughlaq, Muslim plunder of men and materials could not reach Delhi from Devagiri because of the "robbers" on the way.[71] The power of the Jats went on increasing as that of the Mughals declined. Churaman's descendants ruled at Bharatpur till the abolition of princely States in independent India.[72]

Armed opposition to temple destruction by Aurangzeb at Mathura and Varanasi was not quite possible locally because of the might of the Mughal. It was offered in Rajputana, Malwa, Bundelkhand and Khandesh, which were remote from the centre of imperial authority and even there only when the emperor was not present. Later on, when imperial power declined, we read of reprisals in the second half of the reign by certain Rajput and Maratha chiefs, who demolished converted mosques in retaliation, or stopped the *azan* (call to prayer) in their localities. In some places the *jizyah* collector was expelled after plucking out his beard. The terror inspired by an autocratic regime was not easy to overcome. But there did exist an opposition strategy: it was to express resentment and organise armed resistance in places situated far off from the centre of imperial power. And this scenario was not confined to Aurangzeb's reign or Jat peasantry, "although the first extensive outbreak of Hindu reaction against this policy of persecution took place among the sturdy Jat peasantry of the Muttra district."[73] Throughout the medieval period the policy

70 Sarkar, op. cit., p. 400.

71 Barani, p. 502.

72 Sarkar, op.cit., pp. 160-161, 397-400; C.H.I., IV, pp. 243, 245-246, 305, 336.

73 C.H.I., IV, p. 243.

of Muslim rulers was clear and definite and those who responded to it with equal determination were those who today are called scheduled castes, scheduled tribes and other backward castes. They strove by themselves under the leadership of their own chieftains, seeking at the same time the support of Zamindars, rulers and saints of all classes and castes.

For, by the sixteenth century the resistance potential of the Rajputs had been well-nigh exhausted. They had fought against Muslim aggression from the seventh century onwards with determination that evokes our admiration. But in the process, the flower of their youth had more or less perished — young men in wars and young women in *jauhars*. That is why they decided to renounce the path of confrontation and opted out for conciliation under Akbar. This too proved harmful for them. They embroiled themselves in fighting on behalf of and for the glory of the Mughals. Besides, imitation of the Mughal luxurious life sapped their strength. In these circumstances, the leadership of the freedom struggle against Muslim rule in the seventeenth century could not be taken up by the high caste Rajputs.[74] It now rested with the backward classes, mainly the Jats, the Marathas and the Sikhs.

In spite of the Jats' antecedents as a backward community throughout the medieval period, Suraj Mal rose to the position of a Raja and he spearheaded the freedom struggle in the Agra-Mathura region. The Marathas were also counted among backward

---

74 But whenever they found a chance, they helped the resistance movement of the lower classes in order to wreak vengeance against their enemies. For instance, in 1654 emperor Shahjahan sent an expedition to coerce Raja Prithi Shah of Garhwal with his capital at Srinagar. An earlier attempt in 1635 under the governor of Kangra had ended in disaster. A second expedition, conducted with more discretion, also overran the Dun Valley, "hunting down the peasants who fled from their homes and massacring them". The third expedition caused Raja Pirthi Shah to send his son to the Mughal court to offer submission. But he did not forget his humiliation and the suffering of his subjects. When Dara Shukoh's eldest son, Sulaiman Shukoh, sought refuge with the Raja of Srinagar in the Garhwal hills, the latter delivered the fugitive to Aurangzeb. Later on, the Raja of Garhwal assisted Banda Bahadur to escape from the attack of the army of Bahadur Shah I in 1710 (Sir Richard Burn in C.H.I., IV, pp. 207, 227-28, 323; *Imp. Gaz.*, United Provinces of Agra and Oudh, II, p. 280).

castes. They "deserted the plough for the sword in the time of Jahangir."[75] Shivaji was a Kunbi. He belonged to a low caste but was readily accepted all over India as Chhatrapati. Maratha power north of the Vindhyas was witnessed in 1718 when they were invited by one of the factions at the court of Farrukh Siyar. By 1729, they had established themselves in Bundelkhand. The rank and file of the Sikhs were also drawn from the backward castes. The first uprising of the Sikhs took place in 1709, when they invaded Saharanpur and poured into Muzaffarnagar.

In this struggle for freedom from Muslim rule, some tribes and castes suffered decimation. Some others like the Bhils and the Gonds grew in numbers but lost in status. The Jats also registered a demographic rise. They are found in large numbers all over northern India — in Punjab, Rajasthan, Haryana and Delhi in particular.[76] Sikhs and Marathas are now considered as the martial segments of Hindu society.

A special mention of Jats, Marathas, and Sikhs is necessary in this regard. The Jats were the first to face the Muslim onslaught under Muhammad bin Qasim. They are spoken of with contempt by Muslim chroniclers. They continued their resistance to Muslim rule for a thousand years with persistent tenacity. They have not only survived but have made progress in every sphere of national activity. The Marathas had ceased to be a power in the Deccan early in the fourteenth century; they were not a great power even before that. But their struggle against the Muslims regimes was so tenacious that they were called 'mountain rats' and 'naked starved rascals'[77] by Muslims in fear and contempt. At the end of the medieval period, the Marathas were one of the great peoples who helped destroy Muslim rule in India. They spread out in most parts of northern India and form

---

75 *Imp. Gaz.*, Central India, p. 22.

76 *Imp. Gaz.*, Rajputana, pp. 15, 241, 173, 322-23; *Imp. Gaz.*, Punjab, I, pp. 282, 397.

77 John Fryer used this phrase for the Marathas in the seventeenth century. Irfan Habib repeats it more than once on a single page in his book, *Agrarian System of Mughal India*, pp. 350-51.

a determined and virile people today. The Sikhs became great by fighting the Mughals. There was no torture that was not inflicted on them by the Mughals, and yet they rose in strength and stature as the war with the Muslims went on. Today they have made progress in every sphere of life — commercial, educational, scientific. These 'low caste' people developed the strength of steel through their struggle against the Muslims.

Jani Shikar of the Oraons

Like the Gonds in the central and the Jats in the western part of the country, many other tribes opposed oppression in eastern India also. Only the history of their struggles is not easy to reconstruct. Nonetheless it is preserved in their local traditions and it shows that many Rajas as well as tribal people of Assam, Bengal, Bihar and Orissa made their contribution to the preservation of their religion and way of life in these parts through persistent resistance.

In medieval times, the countryside of Orissa was full of forests in which elephants abounded. Firoz Tughlaq marching through Orissa attacked the reigning king Bhanudeva III at which the country was thrown into confusion. "Some of the inhabitants were made prisoners, others fled to the hills." Those who escaped into the wilds remained there for long, probably for all time in future. For, the Sultan spent two years in his Bengal-Orissa campaign during which time there was no possibility of the return of the fugitives. They must have added to the number of tribals by joining them because Orissa had a very large tribal population since earliest times. On its return journey, the Sultan's army "ascended and descended mountains after mountains and passed through jungles and hills until they were quite in despair and utterly worn our with the fatigues of the arduous march."[78]

In the long narrative of Shams Siraj Afif concerning Firoz Tughlaq's invasion of Jajnagar or Orissa, three facts stand out

78 Afif, pp. 165-72; portions trs. in E. D., III, pp. 312-16; Farishtah, I, p. 147; Badaoni, Ranking I, p. 329.

prominently. One, Orissa was a strong and prosperous Hindu kingdom in the fourteenth century. Two, it was full of hills and forests. Three, Muslim armies found it difficult to negotiate them while local people could easily seek shelter in them.

Up to the time of Akbar this situation did not change much. Abul Fazl writes: "From the time that India was conquered (by Muhammadans), none of the (Muslim) princes had raised its standard over Orissa. The rulers of that country had always been powerful. For, on the borders thereof there were dangerous passes and lofty mountains, and heights and declivities innumerable, and difficult forests so that the grasping hand of princes could not reach it..."[79] Later on, the Sur Afghans did away with the Raja of Orissa and sacked the temple of Jagannath.[80]

Akbar determined to oust his Afghan enemy from Bihar and Orissa. In 1590, rebellion in Bengal, Bihar and Orissa was crushed by the Mughal army under Raja Man Singh. "The great Hindu landholders, encouraged by the many Muslim (Afghan) rebels, who yet remained in arms, had ceased to pay revenue."[81] Order was first restored in Bihar, and Raja Man Singh marched through Jharkhand-Chota Nagpur-Bhagalpur route into Orissa. He defeated the Afghan chiefs in Orissa and annexed the country in 1592. The new province, although imperfectly subdued, was attached to the Subah of Bengal.[82] But its peace was gone for good. The resisters took to the wilds at will or when pushed into them by circumstances. (Today most of the Chota Nagpur and large parts of Bihar are tribal areas.) Under Jahangir and Shahjahan the Mughal power remained established but not entrenched. That is how during Shivaji's escape from the Mughal court his movements could be traced only up to Benaras. Thereafter, he "continued his flight by way of Bihar, Patna and Chanda, which is a thickly wooded country and difficult of

79 A.N., II, p. 381.
80 Ibid., pp. 479-80.
81 Wolseley Haig in C.H.I., IV, p. 139.
82 Smith, op. cit., p. 178.

passage".[83] The tribal people of Bihar-Orissa region continued to fight the Mughals as their festival of *Jani Shikar* celebrated by the Oraons, bears witness.

The Oraons are mainly found in Chota Nagpur and Santhal Parganas. They are also known as Kol, which is a generic name applied to Munda, Ho, and Oraon tribes of the region. Oraon is an aboriginal Hindu tribe whose home is in Ranchi. They have their own developed culture.[84] From the early twentieth century, the Oraons have even abandoned their tribal language in favour of a localised Hindi.[85] Dr. Prakash Oraon, Director of Bihar Tribal Research Institute (BTRI), Ranchi, says that *Jani Shikar* is a centuries' old tribal ritual which has now been converted into a *mela* (fair). Som Singh Munda, a research officer at the same institute, says that the *Jani Shikar* must have first taken place around 1610, in the reign of Jahangir. It is held every twelve years. So go on adding 12 years in 1610, till it brings us to 1994, the current year of *Jani Shikar*. "Tradition has it that when the Mughals attacked the Oraons in Rohtas, the women had to take up arms as their menfolk were too drunk celebrating a victory over the Mughals. Ever since, the tribal women, especially the Oraons, celebrate the occasion by setting out from their village on shikar."[86]

The Oraons believe that the Mughals pushed them away from Rohtasgarh into Chota Nagpur. "The *jani shikar* legend is linked with that part of Oraon history. The Mughals were tipped off that the best time to conquer the Oraons was immediately after *sarhul*, when all the males would be drunk after the festivities. An attack was launched. But the Mughals had to beat a hasty retreat. They attacked twice more and had to retreat both the times." Since then the victory of the Oraons over the Mughals is celebrated in the form of *Jani Shikar*. The date of the origin of the ritual suggests a connection, though not certain in context, between the repression of the Mughals

83 Khafi Khan, *Muntakhab-ul-Lubab*, II, p. 219.
84 *Imp. Gaz.*, Bengal, I, pp. 248-51.
85 Ibid, II, pp. 350-51.
86 'Tribal Women Hunters', *The Times of India*, New Delhi, 11-6-1994.

under Jahangir and the resistance of the tribal people of Bihar.

"Every twelve years, in the month of 'jeth' (May-June), the *parha rajas*, confer and decide on the date for launching the '*jani shikar*'. The decision is announced in the villages. On the fixed date, the females dressed in male's attire, with traditional weapons, first seek the blessing of 'pahan', the village priest, and go out for hunting. They also report to the *pahan* first after returning from the *shikar.*

"In fact, as Som Singh Munda says, the *pahan* plays the role of a referee. And no one is allowed to violate the rules. Like, when the *jani shikaris* approach a village, the *pahan* of that village arranges a feast for them. But if he cannot, for any reason, then he blows a whistle, which allows the *shikaris* to roam freely in his village and make their killing. And no complaints are entertained against such killings.

"Like a relay race, the *jani shikaris*' forays last, till they reach the next village. A group from that village takes over from there. Often, different groups hunt together, like they did this year at Morabadi, where '*shikaris*' from Hatma, Kanke and other places assembled.

"One huntress from every house in a village is the norm. If someone cries off then a fine is imposed: a feast, or a goat, or even monetary fine. And these days females from almost all tribes participate in this 12-yearly ritual says Mr. Munda.

"...But, this year, *jani shikaris...* were stopped at Bargain Basti. The village, dominated by minorities, did not allow them fearing the loss of their livestock.

"That was not the isolated case this year...

"[Some] policemen allegedly roughed up a group of *jani shikaris* in the Doranda area. Women living in the area had protested against the stealing of their livestock. The tribal women had justified their action by claiming that they would fall ill if they ignored the ritual."[87]

---

87 'Oraon women go on a legendry hunt' by Arun Kumar Thakur, *The Times of India,* New Delhi, 19-6-1994.

There is no written record of this ritual. But it has gone on through the centuries. Of course, with the passage of time, customs and habits have changed. These days, instead of wearing the traditional male dresses like *pugri* and *dhoti*, the *jani shikari* women prefer hats, sun-glasses, shirts and pants. Martial fairs are held in tribal areas throughout the country, commemorating some unremembered victory, celebrating some unnamed success. *Jani Shikar* is only one of such fairs.

Reddis defend Andhra Country

In encounters between the Muslim regime and tribal resisters, the Kshatriyas used to come to the rescue of low castes and vice versa. An example from the earliest times of Muslim occupation is when in 1195 CE the Mher tribe of Ajmer rose in revolt. The Chaulukyas of Gujarat came to their assistance. Qutbuddin Aibak had to call reinforcements from Ghazni to meet the challenge. He pushed on to Gujarat where he created much havoc and on return to Ajmer destroyed the Sanskrit College of Vishaladeva.

Conversely, there is a rather touching instance of Shudras taking over the defence of their kingdom after the defeat and dispersal of their Kshatriya masters by the Muslims. "In an inscription, dated A.D. 1345, the Reddi dynasty of Andhra describes how after the elimination of the Kshatriya defenders, the duty of defending cows and Brahmins fell on the Shudras, 'born out of the feet of Vishṇu'." The first independent Reddi king Vema "restored all the *agrahāras* [gifts, especially of land] of the Brahmanas, which had been taken away by the wicked Mleccha kings".[88] Another inscription of the same dynasty proudly proclaims Vema's birth from "the victorious fourth *varṇa*, which 'sprang from the feet of Vishṇu'," and which ruled "the remainder of the territory once ruled by the *dvijas* [before the Muslim conquest]", and describes how his first son Anna-Vota gave

88 J. Ramayya, 'Madras Museum plates of Vema' in *Epigraphia Indica* VIII (ASI Reprint, 1981), p. 9.

agraharas to the Brahmanas and how his second son Anna-Vema freed the country from the "crowd of enemies" and used his wealth to sponsor "men of learning".[89] In general, inscriptions of Shudra dynasties declare time and again that belonging to the fourth *varṇa* was a matter of pride for them. What they do not say, but which is equally significant, is that their rule was popular among the Hindus and that they were respected by the people. The Shudras take it as their proud duty to defend the country against the Muslims and uphold the Brahminical culture. An inscription of Singaya-Nayaka (CE 1368) clearly proclaims this pride in belonging to the low castes.[90] Another inscription narrates how his relative, Kapaya Nayaka, "rescued the Andhra country from the ravages of the Mohammedans".[91]

These instances are from the South. In the North the Shudra struggle against the Muslims was perennial. So much so that the "Bhangi confederacy one of the great Sikh sections (of Jats who were habituated to taking *bhang* or hemp) attacked and conquered Ferozepur under their leader, Gujar Singh, who made over the newly acquired territory to his nephew Gurbakhsh Singh (1763)".[92] In the East the exploits of the Oraons and in the West of Meo and Gujar tribes bring into clear focus the part played by the Shudras and Dalits in keeping up a continual struggle against the foreign invaders and rulers. And this struggle enjoyed wide approval of all castes.

---

89 E. Hultzsch, 'Vanapalli plates of Anna-Vema' in *Epigraphia Indica* III (ASI Reprint, 1979), pp. 64-65.

90 K. Rama Sastri, 'Akkalapundi grant of Singaya-Nayaka, Saka-Samvat 1290' in *Epigraphia Indica* XIII (ASI Reprint, 1982), p. 259 ff.

91 Ibid., quoted on p. 261. The above cases together with references of inscriptions have been taken from Koenraad Elst., *Indigenous Indians,* pp. 384-85.

92 *Imp. Gaz.,* Punjab, I, p. 440.

VI
Contribution of Backward Castes to Hindu Society

Castes as Mini-Religions

Many modern politicians keep busy trying to divide Hindu society into tribal, backward and forward castes. The excuse put forward for this exercise is that the upper castes have exploited and oppressed the lower castes for years and that now the latter should extricate themselves from the clutches of the former and avenge the injustice done to them for centuries. In medieval times at least, as seen in a separate section earlier, all high and low castes of Hindus lived under the expansive umbrella of Hindu Dharma or civilization. Of course, each tribe and caste maintained its distinctive personality and followed its special set of rules and conventions. This idea may best be elaborated in the words of Professor Bhikhu Parekh: "Castes are not just occupational and economic units but long established communities with their own distinct moral codes, customs, cultural life, rituals, traditions, sentiments and loyalties... Institutions do not die as long as they continue to meet important needs... Castes continue to exercise considerable influence... because they meet important needs... Though largely illiterate, Hindus are great survivors. Not surprisingly they have used, manipulated, modified, or held firmly to different aspects of the caste system as their vital interests required."[1] In the words of Ram Swarup, "caste represented the principle of security and continuity — one was employed as soon as one was born; it represented the principle of vocation, of training, of excellence, of pride, of dedication; it represented the principle of co-operation, conciliation, culture and dignity; it was also a centre of national power and national expression. It is very

1 Bhikhu Parekh, 'Wisdom of the Caste System', *The Times of India*, New Delhi, 3-4-91.

much later that caste developed negative characteristics. It is only a recent phenomenon when under a different ideological conditioning one caste is maligned in the name of another, and caste is used by powerful vested interests for the fragmentation of society... In old India, all people and castes united in defending their society, in defending temples, Brahmins and cows — still worthy objects of protection by a great compassionate people and civilization... There was a time when caste system was not static and castes often rose and fell in social status. It was also the time when no caste was 'depressed' though there were social differences. Castes became static and depressed during the period of a protracted foreign rule."[2]

All tribes and castes are thus like mini-religious groups comprising the corpus of Hinduism. They have remained attached to their caste or "tribal religion" with as much zeal as has been done by Buddhists, Jains and even Muslims or Christians. Islam is a religion of written rules. Tribes and castes are "religions" of unwritten rules. The conventions or rules of a tribe and caste are both lenient and rigorous and they exhort or compel its members to behaviour consistent with its order and security. Give a choice to the Chamars to become Brahmanas; they will not do so. Give the Brahmanas the option to become Vaishyas or Shudras; they will not. That is how Chamars, Kahars, Koris, Pasis, the Bhils, the Gonds, the Kolis, the Koches have remained attached to their "religions", their unwritten codes of conduct, like the Brahmanas, the Kshatriyas and the Vaishyas. But at the same time they have been and are part of the all protecting and all pervading Hindu civilization. If we count the tribes and castes as "religions" like Buddhism, Jainism, Sikhism and Indian Muhammadanism, we will be able to appreciate why the caste system is so entrenched, why it has not gone in spite of the attempts of so many "reformers", and still why its adherents have remained inalienable part of Hinduism through the ages.

One reason that has kept the faith of the adherents of these

---

2 Ram Swarup in his *Anusmriti and Anudhyāyana* (unpublished).

mini-creeds confirmed in Hindu civilization is the fact that high caste Hindus did not treat the lower caste people as slaves. There is no slavery among Hindus as is found among Muslim and Christian peoples.[3]

Untouchability

Then what about untouchables and untouchability? It is not possible to ascertain precisely the origins of the custom of untouchability. But one thing is known: in the medieval times the Hindus considered all those who ate the flesh of cows as untouchables. This abhorrence of beef was mainly expressed in the practice of not drinking water offered or even touched by the untouchable who was invariably treated as outcaste.

The eleventh century Arab savant Alberuni says that ancient Aryans ate beef. At the same time, he says that Hindu laws are open to change, "for they say that many things which are now forbidden were allowed before the coming of Vasudeva, e.g. the flesh of cows".[4] So, according to Alberuni, beef-eating was prevalent among ancient Hindus but it was given up by them about the time of the Mahabharata. But once it was renounced, it was completely stopped. And all those who ate beef or allied foods like meat, fish, poultry and pork, began to be treated as outcastes and untouchables. These included Alberuni's Antyajas. Antyajas were treated as untouchables as they comprised fishermen and hunters of wild animals and birds. Many others "are not reckoned amongst any caste or guild. They are occupied with dirty work, like the cleansing of the villages and other services. They are considered as one sole class, and distinguished by their occupation. The worst of all are Bhadatau(?) who not only devour the flesh of dead animals, but even of dogs and other beasts."[5] So from Chandalas to Mahabrahmans (or Brahmans who supervise cremation rites), those who ate beef or any other kind of meat or flesh or "who were occupied with dirty work like

3 See Lal, *Muslim Slave System in Medieval India*, esp. pp. 4-6, 17-24, 41-59.
4 Alberuni, I, p. 107.
5 Ibid., pp. 101-102.

the cleansing of the villages", began to be treated as untouchables and outcastes, the two words being used synonymously.

The earliest reference to this custom in the medieval period is found in Al Kufi's *Chachnama,* when, during the first Muslim invasion of Sindh by Muhammad bin Qasim, Rani Bai, the queen of Raja Dahir, exhorting her compatriots to embrace the flames of *jauhar*, exclaimed, "God forbid that we should owe our liberty to those outcaste cow-eaters. Our honour would be lost".[6] Thereafter, during the next thousand years of Muslim occupation and rule there are scores of references to the fact of treating all Hindu and Muslim beef-eaters as being *mlechhas* and untouchables. The Christians were treated likewise. Niccolao Manucci, writing in late seventeenth century, says that "the Hindus account all Europeans to be Pariahs, since they eat cows' flesh, or, in other words, are the very lowest caste or tribe, men with whom they cannot eat..."[7] He says that "The Hindus call all Europeans *Farangis*... They hold the *Farangis* abominable and very dirty... They would sooner die unaided than drink a cup of water from the hand of a *Farangi.*"[8]

Ishtiaq Husain Qureshi expresses shock that the "very touch of the (unclean) Muslim polluted the food of the twice-born Brahman... but praise cannot be withheld from the conquering race for their tolerance in cheerfully submitting to this humiliation".[9] There was no humiliation meant; the Hindus dared not humiliate Muslims during Muslim rule. They did not mean to humiliate anybody — Muslim or Hindu. Beef-eating was at the bottom of untouchability and Muslims had to accept it as did the others. Hindus in general and Brahmanas in particular were not prepared for any compromise on this issue.[10] No one was out of its purview — Hindus, Muslims, or Christians — so that Qureshi himself admits that "it must be remembered that this treatment

6 *Chachnama*, E.D., I, p. 172.
7 Mannucci, III, pp. 319-20.
8 Ibid., p. 73.
9 Qureshi, *Administration of the Sultanate of Delhi,* pp. 227-228.
10 Manucci, III, pp. 310-311.

was not limited to the Muslims." However, any pressure on the part of 'the conquering race' to habitate Brahman localities with meat-eaters met with matching resistance. "Above all others," writes Manucci, "the priests, called Brahmans... will not tolerate those who eat flesh or fish. Anything opposed to the above-named custom is likely to upset everything... there may be a total desertion of their homes by these people, who go where they find themselves better treated, and are allowed to live peacefully in accordance with their customs, without any constraint or force... That was why the Hindus increased the number of their processions, their ceremonies, and their superstitions, by way of invoking the aid of their gods against such treatment which counted with them as violence".[11] Like the Brahmanas, "the baniyas (also) eat neither flesh nor fish". They worship the cow. "Not only the baniyas who thus reverence the cow, but also the whole of the Hindus of whatever station in life".[12] No wonder such "vegetarian" people, who are "full of charity for animals", treated beef and meat eaters as outcastes and untouchables. That is why Manucci does not criticise the Hindus for this custom. On the contrary, he credits them with excellent qualities in this very context. "These Indian peoples esteem above everything else that moral value of gentleness and those who possess it. This is the reason of their having an aversion to the opposite quality..."[13]

So, the vegetarian Hindus in general and Brahmanas in particular treated as untouchables all those who ate beef, pork, fish, and flesh of dead animals and were engaged on cleansing work. The Hindus lowest classes, who partook of such food, accepted untouchability as a matter of custom or convention. There was punishment prescribed for those who flouted this law and associated with the untouchables. Manucci, who had resided in the South for many years, writes about Malabar in particular. He says that the man who associated with the Pariahs lost his caste. He could not find a wife within his caste. "He cannot be received

11 Ibid., III, pp. 310-11, 316-19.
12 Ibid., I, pp. 155-56.
13 Ibid., III, p. 319.

in anyone's house, none may eat or drink with him, cannot even serve him or help him in his necessities, even were he at the very point of death. The rule is so strict that he must either renounce marriage or take a Pariah wife. In short to become a Pariah, he and all his posterity..."[14]

The practice of untouchability, of not touching water or food from a Pariah or outcaste continued throughout the medieval period. The Hindu Kahars, for example, who supplied water in Muslim households, would themselves not drink water touched by Muslim members of the same house. In our own times we have seen that all beef-eaters, all Muslims, all Englishmen from the Viceroy down to the District Collector, were treated as untouchables by their Hindus subordinates and servants. Muslims and Christians had developed an understanding of the institution and had adapted themselves to it. They engaged Hindus *khidmatgars* for buying grocery and doing other outdoor errands, and employed Muslim *khansamas* for cooking meat and beef. Hindu untouchables continued to be treated as outcastes. Since they were mostly poor, their miseries are attributed mainly to untouchability 'imposed by caste Hindus'. Modern Indian society prohibits the practice of untouchability through law. But Hindu abhorrence of beef persists and with it untouchability, not only for Hindu outcastes but also for Muslims and Christians. For Hindus are the one people who have not lost touch with their moorings and roots.

Concern of Caste for Caste

It was, however, not at the root of Hindu civilization to ill-treat the weak. But for untouchability, there is a sensitive concern of the high castes for the low and vice versa. Even when there were wars between Rajputs and lower caste people for possession of land and forts, the former did not cruelly treat those whom they defeated in war or ousted from their lands. For example, in Amber (modern Jaipur) Minas reside in large numbers.

14 Ibid., p. 320.

The Minas had held a good part of this country in the twelfth century. They were dispossessed of it by the Kachhwaha Rajputs. But this unhappy situation was turned into an honourable compromise. It became customary for a Mina to mark the *tika* on the forehead of a new chief of Amber.[15] Jats were also in power in Bikaner State. They voluntarily submitted to Rao Bika on the condition that the Rajput chief was to receive the *tika* of inauguration from a Jat. To this day the headman of Godara Jats applies "unguent of royalty to the forehead of Bikas' successors".[16] The Jats to this day form the most numerous caste in Bikaner; they are now all agriculturists.

Similarly, the Bhils. They were great fighters, not easy to control. They are often mentioned as foes or allies in the history of Anhilwara, and they preceded the Rajputs (and later Musalmans) at Ahmedabad, Champaner, and parts of Rajasthan. It was, however, necessary for the recognition of Rajput chiefs in Mewar, Dungarpur and Banswara till the fifteenth century that they should be marked on the brow with a Bhil's blood.[17] "Rampura (town in Indore State) derives its name from a Bhil Chief, Rama, who was killed by Thakur Sheo Singh Chandrawat of Antri, in the fifteenth century. As a sign of their former sovereignty, the descendants of Rama still fix the *tika* on the forehead of the chief of Chandrawat family (of Malwa)."[18] Such a phenomenon is unique in world history.

That is how commoners and tribesmen remained devoted to their rulers, even though a few of them were sometimes dispossessed or harmed by the latter. They fought shoulder to shoulder with their new masters to save their country and religion against an implacable foe like the invading Muslims. In the present-day mindset, it is an inerasable fixture that high caste Hindus have oppressed low caste people "for centuries". This impelled me to search for evidence. I could not find any information or testimony.

15 *Imp. Gaz.*, Rajputana, pp. 240-41.
16 Ibid., pp. 401-402.
17 *Imp. Gaz.*, Central India, pp. 81-85.
18 Ibid., p. 235.

There is no evidence available in the medieval chroniclers at least that high caste Hindus ever oppressed low caste tribals or backward castes. In modern times of media exposure people read about inter or intra caste conflicts, say between Dalits and others, with consternation. In media-lacking medieval times people would not know about such happenings. Even if they did come to know of any incident, they considered it to be the concern of the respective caste elders or their *panchayats.* It was nobody else's business. Such typical Hindu attitude is of non-interference and tolerance rather than of oppression of caste by caste.

Of course, the feeling of pride in one's caste was surely there. And curiously enough it was more pronounced among lower castes than in the upper. Caste has an hierarchical structure, and even low caste people feel proud of being superior to some other lower castes. Thus a Teli feels himself superior to an Ahir, an Ahir to a Chamar, a Kahar to a Pasi, and so on. Leave aside Yadavs and Kurmis, even a Kori or Teli will not accept water from the lowest caste, for instance, from the Dom. But the Dom too took pride in his caste. About the Dom, sometimes also called Chandal, H. H. Risley says that he will eat the leavings of others, but "no Dom will touch the leavings of a Dhobi, nor will he take water... or any sort of food or drink from a man of that caste... Pods or Chasi, a fishing, cultivating and landholding caste of lower Bengal will eat the leavings of Brahman, but Vaishnava Pods abstain from all kinds of flesh. Rajbansi, a synonym for Koch, wear sacred thread in Bihar."[19] In fact, the lower caste people are more particular about caste pride or "caste preservation" than even the higher caste ones, and "the Hadi", as per Alberuni, "keep themselves free from everything unclean".[20]

The dimensions of this prejudice cannot be precisely appraised. Islam lays down clear rules of conduct for its followers: how Muslims should behave with Muslims, how Muslims should behave with non-Muslims, how they should treat slaves, women

19 H.H. Risley, *The Tribes and Castes of Bengal,* Calcutta, 1891.
20 Alberuni, I, pp. 101-102.

etc. There are no such rules for Hindus. There are literary and religious works like those of Manu and the *Shāstras* which at places advocate discriminatory treatment of low castes. This cannot be denied nor the fact of actual prejudice in day to day dealings. But how much exploitation or repression there was in actual practice is difficult to find out. In Hindu society, exploitation and liberality, repression and condonation, untouchability and fight against untouchability have gone on confusedly intermixed for centuries. For example, the sweeper being untouchable was not touched, but the sweepress was and is more often than not addressed as *bua* or *amma*.[21] The mindset of upper-caste/backward caste conflict syndrome needs reviewing as it is neither based on historical evidence nor supported by compulsions of the situation.

There are two common complaints covered by this syndrome. One is that high caste Hindus are responsible for the exploitation and stark poverty of the backward castes. The other is that high caste Hindus deny entry of Harijans into temples. The two issues need not be mixed up; they may be treated separately.

About the poverty of the low castes enough evidence has been set forth in the foregoing pages to show that it was the policy of the Muslim rulers to impoverish the peasants who

21 An instance from the freedom struggle against British rule in modern times may help in comprehending the situation in the medieval period. In the late 1920s there was a bomb factory at Jhandewalan in Delhi installed by some freedom fighters like Dr. Bapu Ram, S. H. Vatsyayan, Vimal Prasad Jain, Vaishampayan and others, who pretended to manufacture cosmetics. A sweeper woman named Asharfi used to come every day to clean the factory premises. When the existence of the factory was unearthed, the police wanted Asharfi to identify the abovementioned revolutionaries. A sympathiser went to Asharfi's house, touched her feet, called her *maa* and said: "The life of these young men is in your hands, will you give evidence against them?" She said: "I do not know whether the life of the young men is in my hands, but since you have called me *maa*, I will live up to that honour." And she did, despite pressures, inducements and intimidation.

This instance was mentioned by Mr. L.C. Jain, member Planning Commission, in his M.N. Roy Memorial Lecture delivered on March 21, 1991. I am obliged to Mr. Ram Swarup for sending me a copy of the lecture. The so-called low castes have helped the high castes and vice versa at all times, medieval and modern, in hour of need.

formed the bulk of the lower castes, so as to render them incapable of rising against the alien establishment. The artisans too were not paid their due wages by the Muslim nobility as vouched for by Francois Bernier. The French Doctor also noticed that the agriculturists were sometimes so hard pressed that they were forced to leave their lands and seek shelter with some Hindu Raja for passing their days in peace. Many others voluntarily "abandoned the country"[22] and vanished into the jungles. This settles the question as to who was actually responsible for the poverty of the lower castes and who exploited them for centuries — the upper caste Hindus or the Muslim regimes. The backward castes who could not be effectively suppressed by the elaborate apparatus of the Muslim government, could not have possibly been oppressed by the politically powerless Hindu upper castes. But for the Harijans, the backward caste have never been badly treated under the caste system. In fact, among themselves there are, and were in the medieval period, some die-hard sticklers to caste prejudices in rural India. Therefore, those who casually declare that backward castes have been exploited and oppressed by high caste Hindus for centuries would do well to provide evidence for their ill-founded assertion.

About the restriction on the entry of Harijans into temples, a few facts need to be noted. A Hindu temple is not like a Jama Masjid or a Congregation Mosque. Hindu congregational worship or collective religious ceremony like Kumbh or Ardh Kumbh, Jagannath Rathyatra or Ganapati festival are held in wide open spaces. In these no caste restrictions are observed. In Hindu temples the area around the sanctum sanctorum is small because the place is meant for individual worship. Large crowds, holding banners and shouting slogans forcing their entry under the leadership of some modern politician are certainly barred. This of course does not mean that there are no restrictions. Once I (and I am not a Harijan) was not allowed inside a temple at Thiruvanatapuram because I was wearing trousers and not *dhoti*.

22 Bernier, p. 226.

Women devotees between 10 and 50 years of age are not allowed into the Ayappan temple at Sabarimala in Kerala.[23] Foreign women tourists with bare legs are not allowed into mosques. A temple is usually a private shrine. Many, many, Hindu households have small temples in their homes. Except family members no one else can enter them.

All this has not been said to explain away a situation or to exonerate those who refuse entry of Harijans into temples. Such obstructionist people are there even today; they were there in medieval India also. But their number is microscopic. On the other hand, there are hundreds of writers and reformists who are trying to set things right and improve conditions in Hindu places of worship. A good thing is that the Hindu is not allergic to reform; a bad thing is that reforms take a long time to be operative.

Hinduism is a way of life embracing all forms of worship and beliefs including atheism. It does not believe in aggression or violence against heretics (there are no heretics among Hindus) or people of other faiths. It does not believe in forcible conversion of people. This extreme tolerance has its disadvantages: even the slightest malevolence or bigotry on the part of Hindus looks so unnatural that it is always magnified. In the history of other societies, burning the dissenters on the stake, breaking of nonconformists on the wheel, contemptuously calling people of other religions as 'infidels', robbing and massacring them, and terrorizing co-religionists into silence through laws of blasphemy, are considered normal phenomenon. But a hue and cry is made about the so-called ill treatment of lower castes by the

---

23 Recently, when a woman District Collector visited the site (though not the shrine) to oversee the civic amenities there, a debate was sparked off. However, there is provision for worship by all sections — including women and backward castes — nearby. V.J. Thomas writing in *The Times of India*, New Delhi, dated 12-1-95 concludes his report by saying: "Though women between 10 and 50 are not allowed at Sabarimala, there is a temple of a woman deity in its premises. The deity called 'Malikapurathamma' means Goddess sitting on the top of a double-storey building. Sabarimala also has the Temple of backward caste warrior 'Karutha' and the shrine of a Muslim saint Vavar."

upper caste Hindus because such a treatment is just not expected from a Hindu. Absolute freedom leads to anarchy, and some Hindus are social anarchists. Even today some Hindus justify non-entry of Harijans into temples, though their number is one in a million. Even today some people uphold the institutions of *sati*, child marriage and female infanticide but they are one in a million. A few Hindus may not treat the lower castes well, but their behaviour looks atrocious because, unlike other civilizations, Hinduism is expected to be kind and tolerant to all, not only to human beings but even to animals and birds. This situation is also exploited by anti-Hindu Hindus who criticise Hindu social weaknesses no end. This is so because they are secure under its benign roof and know that no *fatwa* (of death) is issued in Hinduism. That is the reason why so much fuss is made about "Hindu atrocities" by anti-Hindus Hindus and non-Hindus.

Reverence for Low Caste Saints

The so-called oppression of the low castes apart, religious leaders and saints belonging to low castes were and are universally respected by all classes of Hindus. The tradition is old and perpetual. Valmiki, the author of the Ramayana, belonged to a primitive tribe. Kamban, who rendered it in Tamil and popularised it, was also from a low caste. Tulsidas's *Rāmacharitmānasa* or Ramayana, is a caste free text, sung with equal devotion by Brahmanas and Harijans alike.

In short, the low caste people freely contributed to the social and religious rejuvenation of Hinduism. The need for such resurrection was the requirement of the besieged Hindu society whose adversaries were determined to destroy it root and branch. While Mullahs[24] and Sufis[25] and Sultans[26] were busy finding ways to

---

24 Ziyauddin Barani, *Sana-i-Muhammadi,* Eng. trs. in *Medieval India Quarterly,* I, Part III, Aligarh, and writings of Shaikh Ahmad Sarhindi, Abdul Quddus Gangohi and Shah Waliullah.

25 A.A.A. Rizvi, pp. 57-58.

26 Actions of Sikandar Butshikan in Kashmir and Sikandar Lodi in Hindustan may be mentioned as instances.

convert the whole country to Islam by leaving to the Hindus a choice only between Islam and death, the Hindus launched their great protestant movement known to history as the Bhakti Movement to save their religion, culture and society. In this movement the highest class Brahmanas and the lowest caste "untouchables" played an equally important role. Indeed some of the leaders of this Bhakti Movement like Sain, Raidas, and Dhanna belonged to the lowest classes of the Hindu social order, while Tukaram was a Vani or low caste trader. But they were as much respected by their contemporary and later Hindu society as any high caste reformers. Raidas or Ravidas was a worker in leather and the people of his family used to do the work of removing carcasses. But this low caste Chamar came to be known as a Sant and Jhali Rani, a princess of Mewar, became his devoted disciple.

The contribution of low caste Bhakti saints to Hindu society is vast and varied. We cannot go into it here in any great detail. To drive home the point we shall make mention of only one or two reformers from the low caste of Chamars, ignoring many others from other low castes. Dadu Dayal lived in the time of Akbar. His family profession was that of a Mochi (tanner or currier) and making of leather bags (*mot*) for drawing water from a well. Dadu spent most of his life in Rajputana and he visited Ajmer, Delhi, Amber and other places where Islamic influence was felt the most. He died at Naraina, a village of the erstwhile Jaipur state, in 1603 CE. In his own time his fame had spread far and wide and he is reported to have had an interview with emperor Akbar himself.[27] A contemporary of Dadu was Birbhan, who founded the famous sect of the Sadhs or Satnamis whom we have met before in their fight against Aurangzeb. They do not observe distinction of caste and rank and abstain from intoxicants and animal foods. Jagjivandas, a Chandel Thakur, either reorganised the old Satnami sect which had suffered defeat from Aurangzeb's armies, or set up a new one with the same name. Dulandas, a disciple of Jagjivandas, who also reorganised the

27 Tara Chand, *Influence of Islam on Indian Culture*, p. 182.

Satnami order, was a Sombansi Kshatriya. Their chief seats are at Delhi, Rohtak in the Punjab, Agra, Farrukhabad and Mirzapur in Uttar Pradesh, and Jaipur in Rajputana. In Central India, Bhandar, a village in the Raipur district, is the headquarters of the Satnami Chamars. Late in the nineteenth century, their leaders Ghasi Das and Balak Das wielded great influence among Ahirs, Kurmis, Telis etc.[28] Kolis, Bhils, and Kathis of Western India were greatly influenced by Sahajananda, the founder of the Swami Narayana sect. He prohibited the killing of animals and the use of animal food or liquor or drugs. He insisted upon strict sexual relations. His priests were celibates. He practised non-violence and taught the doctrine of suffering injury without retaliation.

The point to emphasize here is that from Brahmanas like Chaitanya and Vallabhacharya to low caste people like Kabir (the weaver), Dhanna (the Jat), and Raidas (the Chamar) all saints served contemporary Hindu society with equal fervour and they were all treated with equal respect. They did not raise the bogey of caste. They worked for the integration of society, not for its split. They were not separatists. It may also be pointed out that it is not true that Brahmanas alone hold the post of a high priest in a temple. There have been numerous cases of backward caste devotees being appointed to the post of high priest. As S.V. Desikachar[29] in a recent publication has emphasized, what held ground everywhere through the ages were tradition, custom and usage, and not the lording of high castes over low castes.

Economic Activity

More than in religion, the contribution of the lower castes in the sphere of economic activity in medieval India was significant. Lower castes formed the bulk of the population. They mostly belonged to the bulk of the OBCs of today. They provided food and apparel, services and comforts, to the society in towns and

---

28 Charles Grant, op, cit., pp. 56, 100, 412-13.
29 *Caste, Religion and Country*, New Delhi, 1993.

villages. In urban areas these comprised all kinds of artisans, from basket and rope makers to cloth printers, embroiders, carpet makers, silk weavers, blacksmiths, goldsmiths, tin workers, carpenters, oil-men, barbers, jugglers, mountebanks, street singers, brewers, tailors, betel-leaf sellers, flower sellers, masons, stone-cutters, bullock-cart drivers, *doli* carriers, water carriers, domestic servants, *dhobis* and workers in a hundred other skilled and unskilled crafts.[30] In the villages there lived peasants and shepherds, besides a few artisans of the vocations enumerated above, although of inferior skill.

The quality of work of the urban artisans and craftsmen used to be good. Let us take one example, that of stone-cutters and builders of edifices. Amir Timur or Tamerlane, who invaded Hindustan in 1398, was highly impressed with Indian craftsmen and builders and on his return home from India he took with him architects, artists and skilled mechanics to build, in the mud-walled Samarqand, edifices similar to the Qutb Minar and the (old) Jama Masjid of Delhi constructed by Firoz Shah Tughlaq.[31] Babur also was pleased with the performance of Indian workmen and described how thousands of stone-cutters and masons worked on his buildings in Agra, Sikri, Biana, Dholpur, Gwalior and Koil. "In the same way there are numberless artisans of every sort in Hindustan."[32] Indian workmen belonging to lower castes set up encampment for the army; they worked in *karkhanas* and fabricated weapons and wares. They produced harvests of grains, vegetables, fruits, and flowers; they manufactured butter, sugar, scents, perfumes and gold, silk and cotton stuffs. Upkeep of animals — elephants, camels, horses, cows, mules — and furniture and buildings was in their charge. Hunting, fishing, and selling in the market were their occupations. In short, the Shudras and other lower castes in medieval India had

30 Jaisi, *Padmāvat*, pp. 154, 413; Pelsaert, p. 60; Ashraf, *Life and Conditions of the People of Hindustan*, p. 193.

31 Price, *Memoirs of the Principal Events*, III, p. 267; Percy Brown, *Indian Architecture* (Islamic Period), p. 26.

32 *Babur Nama*, II, pp. 518, 520.

the monopoly of most of the jobs dealing with production such as weaving, dyeing, carpentry, smithy (*lohari, swarankari*), metal-work etc. Medicine and surgery, engineering and agriculture were also mainly with the backward castes. Agriculture in particular was under their exclusive control. They worshipped their tools; their presiding deity was Vishwakarma.

But their economic condition was not good and the extreme poverty of the working classes (the OBCs of today) has not left them till our own times. The reason for this is their exploitation by the Muslim nobles and other elites for not paying the artisans and workmen well. They generally produced goods according to orders placed by their clients. Bazars in the medieval period were not like the markets or shopping centres of today. Ziyauddin Barani describes the bazar of Delhi in the fourteenth century. Most of them were wholesale *mandis*, although there were a few retail shops for the poor also.[33] Babur was not impressed with the markets of Agra and Delhi, nor was Bernier.[34] Akbar probably built a large bazar in his Fatehpur Sikri.[35] Dargah Quli Khan describes Chandni Chowk as the principal bazar of eighteenth century Delhi.[36] Still readymade articles at the shops of rather poor quality were meant for the common people. From all accounts it appears that quality articles needed by Muslim nobles and other elites were prepared by workmen on order by their clients including "the monarch and principal Omrahs". Francisco Pelsaert writes: "For the workmen there are two scourges, the first of which is low wages. Goldsmiths, painters (of cloth or chintz), embroiderers, carpet makers, cotton or silk weavers, black-smiths, copper-smiths, tailors, masons, builders, stone-cutters, a hundred crafts in all — any of these working from morning to night can earn only 5 or 6 *tackas* (*tankahs*), that is 4 or 5 strivers in wages. The

33 Barani, pp. 313 ff.

34 *Babur Nama*, II, p. 518; Bernier, p. 252.

35 R.C. Gaur, 'Medieval Roads and Shops in Fatehpur Sikri', P.I.H.C., 1982, pp. 808-10.

36 *Muraqqa-i-Dihli*, Persian text with Urdu trs. by Nurul Hasan Ansari, Delhi 1982, pp. 129-34, 155-56.

second (scourge) is (the oppression of) the Governor, the nobles, the *Diwan*, the *Kotwal*, the *Bakshi*, and other royal officers. If any of these wants a workman, the man is not asked if he is willing to come, but is seized in the house or in the street, well beaten if he should dare to raise any objection, and in the evening paid half his wages, or nothing at all..."[37]

What Pelsaert writes about Agra in the time of Jahangir, Bernier writes about Delhi in the time of Shahjahan and Aurangzeb. He says that "... grandees pay for a work of art considerably under its value, and according to their own caprice".[38] "When an *Omrah* or *Mansabdar* requires the services of an artisan, he sends to the *bazar* for him, employing force, if necessary, to make the poor man work; and after the task is finished, the unfeeling lord pays, not according to the value of labour, but agreeably to his own standard of fair remuneration; the artisan having reason to congratulate himself if the *Korrah* has not been given in part payment."[39] From these facts the extent of their poverty and nature of their food can be easily inferred. "For their monotonous daily food they have nothing but a little *khichri*... in the day time, they munch a little parched pulse or other grain, which they say suffices for their lean stomachs... Their houses are built of mud with thatched roofs. Furniture there is little or none, except some earthenware pots to hold water and for cooking... Their bedclothes are scanty, merely a sheet or perhaps two..."[40] If this was the situation in the Mughal capitals, Agra and Delhi, the extent of exploitation in other cities was no better if not worse. Writing around the year 1624, Della Valle gives glimpses of life in Surat by pointing out that the people were poor and wages low. But being a centre of trade and manufacture, the royal revenue was considerable. That is why Shahjahan had given to his favourite daughter, Jahanara Begum,

37 Pelsaert, pp. 60-61.

38 Bernier, p. 228. Also Mukerjee, *Economic History of India*, pp. 67-71.

39 Bernier, pp. 256, 288. The *Korrah* was not an ordinary cane. Sometimes a man could be cut into two pieces with its stroke/strokes (Afif, p. 451).

40 Pelsaert, pp. 60-61.

the revenue of Surat for her expenses on betel.[41] A contemporary foreign visitor of Della Valle was John De Laet (1631). He summarised the information he had collected from English, Dutch and Portuguese sources regarding the Mughal empire as a whole. "The condition of the common people," says he, "is exceedingly miserable"; wages are low, workmen get only one regular meal a day, the houses are wretched and practically unfurnished, and people have not got sufficient covering to keep warm in winter.[42]

Like artisans, the condition of other workers was equally bad. Artisans were skilled workmen; peons, servants and shopkeepers were not so and according to Pelsaert their "status differs very little from voluntary slavery". He further says that "peons or servants are exceedingly numerous in this country and every one (soldier, merchant or government official) keeps as many as his position and circumstances permit. Outside the house, they serve for display, running continually before their master's horse; inside, they do the work of the house, each knowing his duty," like the *bailwan,* the *farrash,* the *masalchi,* the *mahawat* etc. Edward Terry (1616-19), Pelsaert and many others note that men stood in the market places to be hired and many of them were paid very low wages or even paid in kind, "for most of the great lords reckon 40 days to the month, and pay from 3 or 4 rupees for that period: while wages are often left several months in arrears, and then paid in worn-out clothes or other things."[43] The weak and the injured could not raise a voice of protest because, says Bernier, "the only law that decides all controversies is the cane and the caprice of a governor".[44]

The story of the exploitation of the poor, both rural and urban, by the Muslim nobles and the elite is unending. And the guiding principle of this pernicious practice was to leave the people with bare subsistence. No foreign traveller fails to notice

41 Manucci, I, pp. 67, 216.
42 Moreland, *India at the Death of Akbar,* pp. 267-69 and n.
43 Pelsaert, pp. 62-63.
44 Bernier, pp. 235-36.

it with disapproval if not disgust. It would appear that the lords and the upper classes in India under Muslim rule derived a cynical pleasure in oppressing the poor. The system of reward and punishment was special. Reward was meant for the rich, punishment for the poor. There are repeated references to rewards and pensions being awarded to Muslim commanders, scholars, Sufis etc., but in the case of the poor, "if a horse lost condition, the fines came down to the water carriers and sweepers employed in the stable. When an elephant died through neglect, the attendants (some of whom drew less than three rupees a month) had to pay the price of the animal."[45] Abul Fazl is all praise for Kahars, or Palki bearers. "They form a class of foot-servants peculiar to India. They carry heavy loads on their shoulders, and travel through mountains and valleys. With their palkis, singhasans, chandols, and dulis, they walk so evenly that the man inside is not inconvenienced by any jolting... At Court several thousands are kept." Their pay, however, was paltry — 192 to 384 pence per head-bearer, 120 to 160 pence for common bearers.[46] Fines are not included in this.

It was not only the low castes, but all classes of Hindus who suffered in the medieval period. The result was that not only peasants but other sections also — artisans, skilled and unskilled labour — took to other ways than concentrating on their work. The hundred years of Mughal rule from Akbar to Shahjahan (1556-1658) is supposed to be the best period in the whole epoch of Muslim rule in India. And it was during this period that conditions were most deplorable. William Hawkins, who was in India during Jahangir's reign, found that "almost a man cannot stir out of doors throughout all his dominions without great forces, for they are all become rabels". The escapers into forest turned highway robbers. Tavernier said that, in about 1660, "to travel with honour in India, one hired 20 to 30 armed men, some with bows

---

45 *Ain*, I, pp. 139, 148-49, 235; Moreland, *India at the Death of Akbar*, pp. 190-91.

46 *Ain*, I, p. 264.

and arrows and others with muskets. They cost Rs. 4 a month".[47] The profession must have been well organised and yet the wages were miserably low.[48]

The Brahmana remained low in economic status although he was respected for his services as a priest, an astrologer and a scholar of scriptures. The Kshatriya was a warrior employing in his service troops of the so-called backward castes. The Vaishya as businessman was well off, but as a scribe he lived from hand to mouth. These higher castes could hardly oppress the lower castes. It is repeatedly said that India is not a Hindu country, that India is and was a multi-religious, multi-cultural state. Surely in the medieval period most of the country was under Muslim rule with its set rules about treatment of non-Muslims. So, when the extreme poverty of the low castes is seen, it should not be forgotten that it was brought about by centuries of Muslim rule. But strangely enough, whenever there is talk of exploitation of the lower castes, only the Hindu is said to have practised it.

It is said that it was Muslims who encouraged if they did not actually introduce the cadre of Churha or Bhangi because of their rules of cleanliness among men and purdah system among women. There is no recorded evidence for this; all that can be said is that Hindu town planning and social customs in ancient India do not suggest the existence of dry latrines inside the house requiring the services of Bhangis. On the other hand, there is also no evidence that Muslims brought civilization to India and raised the country from "the age of savagery to the age of progress", or took any steps to improve the lot of lower castes in the medieval period. Similarly, there is no evidence to show that upper caste Hindus oppressed lower caste Hindus. Indeed, the Indian society got unhinged because of the oppressive tax structure of medieval times when under a top-heavy expenditure-oriented administration in which the salaries of the luxury-loving Muslim nobles rocketed sky-high impoverishing their providers

47 Foster, *Early Travels*, pp. 113, 114; Tavernier, *Travels in India*, I, p. 38.
48 Moreland, *India at the Death of Akbar*, pp. 192-93.

— the lower castes of Hindus suffered as much as the higher ones. It was in the medieval period that the lower castes and tribals inhabiting forest areas were reduced to living a miserable existence.

The scars of self-exile of most of the tribals into forests in the medieval period are difficult to erase. It was in the forests, however, that Oraon, Munda, Kisan, Kherwar, Birjia and Asur did some good work which could not reach out of the forest. The Asur, for example, were the country's first iron smelters. But now Asur and Birjia are on the verge of extinction. Many tribals in the forests alone can locate plants and herbs possessing high medicinal value, but now no one cares to consult them. The scars inflicted on scheduled castes and other backward castes during the same period were equally deep. As the jungle areas are shrinking today, their deplorable huts and habitats are becoming exposed to the eye of 'civilization'. In their jungle village settlements one can only see their naked bodies, their famished children and their empty grain pots. And most people clamp the blame for their extreme poverty on the Hindu upper castes forgetting the ravages wrought under Muslim rule.

In short, the talk about the upper castes oppressing the backward castes "for centuries" is not supported by historical evidence. In the beleaguered Hindu society, the lower castes needed the upper castes as much as the upper castes needed the lower. The lower caste representatives and reformers from Raidas to Ambedkar have always been respected by all sections of Hindu society. Every one of the low castes in medieval India used to work. Every one had his profession or vocation. If he wished to make progress by changing to another craft, he had to work hard to learn it, but there was no hindrance to such 'migration'. The stark poverty of the lower castes today is not due to "centuries of exploitation" by the upper castes but because of the nature and policies of the Islamic state.

Social Mobility of Backward Castes

In the preceding pages we have seen that the Satnamis were

Chamars by caste. Some of their leaders, however, rose to become Kshatriyas and Thakurs. This was upward social mobility or social sanskritization as the sociologists say. Shudras in medieval India in particular used to rise (and fall) with change of circumstances. The Shudras are not mentioned in medieval chronicles, probably because the word 'Shudra' is not easy to transcribe in the Persian script. But Shudra as a generic term was very well known. Any one who was poor or was reduced to poverty through adverse circumstances became a Shudra. Conversely, a Shudra who gained in economic, social or political status used to become a Kshatriya. The number of Kshatriyas was prone to decline because of intra-clan struggles, confrontation with Muslim invaders and rulers, and the expulsion of people from their villages, houses and lands by nobels, governors or *faujdars*.[49] Their resistance and reassertion used to rehabilitate them as Kshatriyas. This upward movement from Shudra to Kshatriya used to replenish their numbers. Social ascendance from Shudra to Kshatriya was common in the medieval period. From the Jats who opposed Muhammad bin Qasim to those who seized Agra and attempted to take Delhi (1763 CE), is one story of a low caste gained in prestige and strength. For centuries the Jats were not counted as Rajputs; they were considered Shudras.[50] But the exertions of Churaman and achievements of Surajmal made Hindu society accord to them the status of Kshatriyas. The most prominent example of this social uplift is that of Shivaji. Wolseley Haig quoting J.C. Grant Duff notes that

---

49 We have seen the part played by the private retainers of *iqtadars* in the Sultanate period in collecting land revenue assigned to them. In the Mughal period such retainers or troopers hired for a temporary period were known as *sih-bandis* or irregular levy. They were not considered eligible for musters and were generally regarded with some contempt when comapared with the regular soldiers or *tabinan*. These quasi-troops behaved like modern lathi-wielding *dadas* employed by their dons to collect revenue or do other police duties. They used to got to any length in perpetrating atrocities on the people reducing them to the status of Shudras in no time (*Babur Nama*, p. 470 and n; *Tuzuk-i-Jahangiri*, I, pp. 8-9; *Tarikh-i-Salim Shahi*, Price, p. 12).

50 P.C. Chandawat, *Mahārājā Sūrajmal aur unkā Yug*, pp. 6-15

Chhatrapati Shivaji, after his "ceremonial enthronement performed other ceremonies which raised him (from a Shudra) to the dignity of a Kshatriya."[51]

On the other hand, there were many high castes which were reduced in status due to adverse circumstances during the medieval times. Take the case of Khangars in the environs of Jhansi. After the defeat of the last great Chandel Raja by Prithvi Raj Chauhan in 1182 CE, and after the raids of Muhammadans under Qutbuddin Aibak in 1202-03 and Iltutmish in 1234, the country lapsed into anarchy. The Khangars, who are said to have been subjects of the Chandels and are now represented by a menial class, held the tract for some time and built the fort of Karar near Orcha.[52] They were superseded who in the thirteenth-fourteenth century by the Bundelas who founded the city of Orcha in 1531. In the Mirzapur district the Bhars once held the valley of the Ganga. Eastward from Chunar the country was held by the Cherus. The Seoris, who are now almost extinct, were formerly powerful. In the south of the district, Kols and Kherwars ruled in the forests. About the end of the twelfth century, Rajput clans seized the whole district, portions of which fell into the hands of the Musalmans a few years later.[53]

Similarly, the town of Chunar was in the hands of Hindus. It was taken by Muslims to be recaptured by Hindus again. "It again fell into the hands of the Muhammadans, though the actual command of the fort remained in the hands of the Bahelias till it became British." Jaunpur "has recently been identified as the fort of Munj captured by Mahmud of Ghazni in 1019". The earliest traditions aver its occupation by the aboriginal Bhars and Seoris. The Bhars still numbered as many as 25,000 at the beginning of the twentieth century.[54] The Bhars who once held the

51 C.H.I., IV, p. 275. Also Jadunath Sarkar, *Shivaji and his Times*, Fourth Ed., 1948, Chapter XVI, and Grant Duff, *History of the Marathas*, I, p. 225.

52 *Imp. Gaz.*, United Provinces of Agra and Oudh, II, p. 87.

53 Ibid., p. 144.

54 Ibid., pp. 155, 159, 162.

these separate designations. They are a very industrious and persevering community, thrifty and frugal." The Kunbi is fond of asserting his independence. They changed from cultivators to warriors and vice versa as per need. Since vocational openings in medieval India were limited, the change of profession was mainly from Kisan to Jawan. During the wars of Aurangzeb with the Bijapur and Golkunda kingdoms, the Kurmis and Kunbis enlisted in the Mughal army. Aurangzeb considered the Dakhini (Maratha) soldiers as "the bravest and most enterprising in India".[61] Since their disbandment after the death of Aurangzeb, they settled down as peaceful cultivators. When the Marathas marched into the North to conquer and spread their rule, the Kunbis took to arms again and became the renowned Maratha warriors.

Conclusion

The tribal as well as non-tribal populations of India have lived in this country since the dawn of civilization. In the medieval period, in particular under Muslim rule, their numbers and nomenclatures multiplied due to natural process of procreation and addition of refugees from the tyrannies of government and nature. But they were all united against odds which affected them adversely. They all lived and desired to live under the benign and wide umbrella of Hindu civilization.

Now certain interested quarter are trying to separate the tribals and "other backward castes" from Hindu society.

A section of the Scheduled Castes has organized itself in the Dalit (or "oppressed") movement. In itself it should present no problem. But in the Dalit literature there is a manifest streak of negativism and breast-beating, and the Hindu upper castes are called wolves and exploiters.[62] And this Dalit current is receiving active support of subversive forces including the Christian missionary establishment. Its anti-Hindu stance is proving divisive

---

61 Manucci, III, p. 306.

62 Koenraad Elst, *Indigenous Indians*, p. 261.

and detrimental to the unity of the country, because "Hinduism is the only thing which keeps India together".[63]

Brahmanas, Kshatriyas, Kayasthas, Khatris, Banias, the hundreds of occupation 'castes', the Shudras and their sub-divisional groups have never fought against each other with sword in hand spilling blood. How can then one believe that all upper castes joined together against the lower castes and oppressed and suppressed them. Hindus had organised their society in a spirit of cooperation and non-violence. This is the crux of Hindu culture. Hindus and Buddhists and Jains live together and worship together. Hindus of various social "strata" lived together in the medieval period without fighting or shedding blood. In times of war unity and cooperation are achieved as a matter of course. They are not automatic or imperative in times of peace. Therefore unity used to elude them now and then. But once they were face to face with perennial war against foreign invaders and rulers, social if not always political unity was automatically forged. High and low, all joined hands to fight the enemy throughout the medieval period.

Yes, caste system was there amongst all Hindus as it is there today — with varied degrees of flexibility. Caste system is prevalent among the tribals also because "the endogamy and exogamy practice of the tribals and Sanskritic Hindus are essentially the same". For example, the Gonds in Bastar have their rules of endogamy. They have their "untouchables" as well. "Highest among the three untouchable groups are...Mahars... Beneath them are the Bhoyars or Malai. At the lowest level are the Magdis. They have their Panchayats (Parha) whose business it is to watch over the interests of the clan and the tribe. In short there has existed an unbroken tribal-Hindu continuum."[64] The attempt by European anthropologists, Christian missionaries and modern politicians to divide them is due to reasons suiting each of them.

63 Kamalini Sengupta, 'Dalit is not a dirty word' in *The Times of India*, New Delhi; 29-1-95.

64 Koenraad Elst, *Indigenous Indians*, pp. 174-204. He refers to many anthropologists and "Fathers" for the above facts.

Medieval Persian chroniclers did not find any distinction between them and describe them all as "Hindus", "Kafirs" or "Robbers". The response of the tribals too was characteristically Hindu. Joseph Troisi observes: "There is a remarkable abhorrence, among the Santals, of the Muhammadans whom they call Turuk, a term which carries a connotation of contempt." Although Muslim traders still do business with the Santals, "the Santals of Pangro, like many other Santals elsewhere...do not accept food from these Muslims".[65]

British rulers thrived on divisions in Indian society. Some modern politicians also thrive on dividing Hindu society. Hence a great deal of noise is made about the 'fact' that caste Hindus have oppressed the tribals, the Dalits and lower castes "for centuries". They see grinding poverty of the poorer classes and attribute it to upper caste Hindu exploitation and oppression. But as seen earlier, all Hindus suffered during the medieval period, the higher castes equally with the lower castes. The high caste Hindus are hardly responsible for the stark poverty of the poor sections. The major question is: If the tribals and low castes were oppressed by high caste Hindus, why did they insist on being counted as Hindus? Once the castes who are being taught to regard themselves as oppressed and suppressed by upper caste Hindus "for centuries", realise that a surreptitious attempt is being made to distinguish and separate them from the main body of Hindus, there will be resentment and reassertion of their identity as Hindus. Hinduism was and has remained their first love.[66]

At the end it may be reiterated that in the crucible of medieval Indian history, hundreds of tribes and castes went up or

---

65 J. Troisi, *Tribal Religion*, 1978, p. 247, cited in Elst, op.cit., pp. 227-28.

66 A news report from Raipur, datelined 13 December 1994, says that over twenty thousand tribal converts to Christianity in Jashpur region have offered to come back to their original faith, Hinduism. They have accepted that their forefathers had converted themselves to Christianity due to temptation and intimidation by Christian missionaries. Shri Dilip Singh Joo Deo, M.P., before whom the tribals had made the offer, said that the British had kept the tribals out of Hinduism by impressing upon them that they (tribals) had no religion. The report further says that it is not conversion, but return to their original faith.

down in social status through political, economic and religious forces operating under Muslim rule. The Jats, the Sikhs and the Marathas went up. The Gonds and the Bhils have remained the same or have gone down in status through the passing of time. In short, there was inter and intra social mobility of tribes and castes throughout the medieval period. A significant point to note is that even the lowest castes had an importance of their own in Hindu society. The cooperation and services of Nai, Dhobi, Kumhar, Kahar etc. were as important as that of the Brahmana Purohit in ages when there were no modern gadgets. The higher castes depended as much on the lower as the lower on the higher. All castes and non-castes were an essential part of the Hindu social and economic order.

As Will and Ariel Durant have pointed out, "A knowledge of history may teach us that civilization is a co-operative product, nearly all peoples have contributed to it; it is our common heritage and debt; and the civilized soul will reveal itself in treating every man or woman, however lowly, as a representative of one of these creative and contributory groups."[67] This applies to Hindu civilization more than any other.

67 Will and Ariel Durant, *The Lessons of History*, New York, 1968, p. 31.

VII
Muslim Army and Backward Classes

Medieval Indian people loved their village, their fields and their homes. Attachment to land was a very strong bond in the medieval world. The Hindus in particular liked to snugly live in their homes under the protection of the joint family system. Only when their homes and fields were threatened without any hope of redemption did they leave their lands. Once uprooted from their homes they migrated to even far off places. Medieval chronicles repeatedly make mention of flight of people into the forests, not of any returnees. And as seen in the preceding pages, those who sought shelter in the wilds turned into Scheduled Tribes, Scheduled Castes and Other Backward Castes. We now know, on the basis of their large population, that the migrations into the wilds in the medieval period were continual and on a large scale.

Principles of War

One major cause of their flight was oppressive tax structure. All Muslim chronicles and kings from Balban to Alauddin Khalji to Shere Shah to Aurangzeb knew that if the peasants were oppressed, they would abandon their lands, and their villages would be ruined. Still they continued to collect as much tax as possible, what if the people even fled from their fields. Another reason of flight was the never ceasing warfare. External invasions by foreign Muslim invaders and internal incursions of Muslim rulers into neighbouring kingdoms were everyday affair. Wars have been there all the time in all parts of the world. These were there in medieval India also. But the wars waged by Muslims were special. They did not wage wars; they mounted *Jihads*. The *Jihad* or 'holy war' is a multi-dimensional concept. It means fighting for the sake of Allah, for the cause of Islam, for converting people to the 'true faith', for destroying their places of worship, for dispossessing them of everything they love. The *Hidayah* lays down that "if the Mussulmans subdue an infidel territory before any capitation tax be established, the inhabitants, together with their wives and children, are all plunder, and the property of the state, as it is lawful to reduce to slavery all *infidels,* whether they be *Kitabees, Majoosees* or *idolaters.*" It also lays down that "whoever slays an infidel is entitled to his [the infidel's] private property,"[1] which invariably included his women and children. Without *Jihad* there is no Islam. *Jihad* is the religious duty of every Muslim. It inspired Muslim invaders and rulers to do deeds of valour, of horror and of terror. Muslim chroniclers have written about the achievements of the heroes of Islam in this regard with zeal and glee.

We need not go into all the ramifications of *Jihad* except those which contributed towards the growth of Scheduled Castes and Scheduled Tribes in India. The first great Muslim who sent Muhammad bin Qasim on the first major invasion of Hind and Sindh was Hajjaj bin Yusuf. He instructed Qasim how to fight *Jihad* with the adversary. "When you encounter the unbelievers," wrote he, "strike off their heads... make a great slaughter among them... (Those who survive) bind them in bonds... grant pardon to no one of the enemy and spare none of them" etc., etc.[2]

Al Hajjaj was a great Jihadist. He was appointed Governor of Mecca in 73 A.H. and of Medina in 74 A.H. (692 and 693 CE) by the Cailiph Abdul Malik. Later, returning to Mecca, Al Hajjaj ordered the reconstruction of the Kaba which had been battered and ruined by the catapults of the Syrian army in 64 A.H. (683). He extended the frontiers of the Ummayad rule over Transoxiana and Sindh. He was a devout Muslim well-versed in Quran, and his exhortations to Muhammad bin Qasim were based on the injunctions of that scripture. In *Surah* (Chapter) 2, *ayat* (injunction) 193, the Quran says, "Fight against them (the *mushriks*)

1 *The Hedaya,* Hamilton (trs.), II, pp. 181, 213.
2 Al Kufi, *Chachmana,* English trs. Kalichbeg, p. 155 and n.

until idolatry is no more, and Allah's religion reigns supreme." The command is repeated in *Surah* 8, *ayat* 39. In *Surah* 69, *ayats* 30-37 it is ordained: "Lay hold of him and bind him. Burn him in the fire of hell." And again: "When you meet the unbelievers in the battlefield strike off their heads and, when you have laid them low, bind your captives firmly" (47.14-15). "Cast terror into the hearts of the infidels. Strike off their heads, maim them in every limb" (8:12). Such commands, exhortations and injunctions are repeatedly mentioned in Islamic scriptures. The main medium through which these injunctions were to be carried out was the 'holy' *Jihad.* And Mohammad bin Qasim followed these injunctions in word and spirit.

But such horrendous ideas were shocking to the Hindus. For, as there were rules regarding *Jihad*, the Hindus also waged wars according to certain rules. The principles regulating wars have been "elaborately described in the *Dharmasutras* and *Dharmasastras*, the epics, the *Arthasastra* treatises of Kautilya, Kamandaka, and Sukra," and not unoften punishment was inflicted on the warrior who did not act up to the regulations laid down.[3] The Mahabharata enjoined that a warrior in armour must not fight with a warrior who was not clad in coat of mail, and cease fighting when the opponent became disabled. The general rule was that warriors should fight only with their equals and should not harm the aged, women, children and those who had surrendered unconditionally.[4] Also fields, gardens, temples and other places of worship were to be left unmolested. All this is testified to by Megasthenes.[5] It is refreshing to note that in Ancient India the Laws of War were designed to bring out the best and not the worst of human nature. Even during the medieval period, as has been observed by K.M. Munshi, "Whatever the provocation, the shrine, the Brahmana and the cow were sacrosanct... harassment of the civilian population during military

3 Dikshitar, *War in Ancient India,* pp. 60-61.

4 Ibid., pp. 67-69.

5 MaCrindle, *Ancient India as described by Megasthenes, Fragment* I, also *Arthashāstra,* Shamashastry's trs., XIII,4.

operations was considered a serious lapse from the code of honour. The high regard which all Kshatriyas had for the chastity of women, also ruled out abduction as an incident of war."[6] Moreover, never in this country was a war psychology developed for aggressive ends. The whole nation was never trained for purposes of war.[7]

On the other hand, the establishment and continuance of Muslim rule in India through *Jihad* was dependent on its army, primarily. Extension of Muslim political power in India was not possible without a formidable war machine, and so the Turkish Sultanate was, by its very nature, committed to maintaining a strong army. The army of the Ghaznavids and Ghaurids, the founders of Muslim rule in India, was a very effective and striking force, as their victories in India show. The army of the Sultanate (1206-1526 CE) was patterned on this prototype; it was almost a continuation of this model. It is, therefore, necessary to study the organisation and functions of the army.

The Men

The army of the Sultanate could be roughly classified into three categories — soldiers in the permanent employment of the ruler, special recruits enrolled on the eve of an expedition, and the volunteers or Ghazis "for no pay but a share in the booty, for participating in what was called a *Jihad*".[8] Ziyauddin Barani rightly calls soldiers of the Sultanate as *Ahl-i-Jihad*.[9]

Soldiers in permanent service were largely drawn from his personal slaves.

Right from the days of Mahmud of Ghazni, the core of the regular army was the slave force (*ghilmān, Mamālik*).[10] These were obtained as presents and part of tribute from subordinate states or enslaved during campaigns. Captured or imported as

6 K.M. Munshi, 'End of Ancient India' in Bharatiya Vidya Bhavan Journal, IV, No. II, December 29, 1959, pp. 8-14.

7 Lal, *Studies in Medieval Indian History*, pp. 120-21.

8 Habibullah, *The Foundation of Muslim Rule in India* p. 262, also p. 265.

9 Barani, pp. 293-94.

10 Minhaj, I, p. 180; C.E. Bosworth, *The Ghaznavids*, p. 98.

youths, they were broken in at an early age, and their minds could be moulded and their bodies trained for warfare. The crucial development of the period from the thirteenth to the fifteenth century was almost the "Universal extension of the Mamluke military system. To sustain the new principalities, slaves, imported as youths from peripheral regions, were trained at the court of their masters to be a fighting and administrative elite loyal to them alone and their comrades in arms."[11] The value of the slave troops lay in their lack of roots and local connections and inculcation of attachment to the new ruler by a personal bond of fealty.

Slaves were collected from all countries and nationalities. There were Turks, Persians, Buyids, Seljuqs, Oghuz (also called Iraqi Turkmen), Afghans, Khaljis, Indians etc., in the army of Mahmud. The success of the Ghaznavids and Ghaurids in India was due, besides other reasons, to the staunchly loyal slave troops.[12] This tradition of obtaining slaves by all methods and from all regions, was continued by the Delhi sultans. In his campaign against Katehar, Balban massacred all male adults and enslaving boys only upto the age of eight or nine. The age factor is significant. As these boys grew in age, they could hardly remember their parentage or nativity, and remained loyal only to the king. No wonder that in the days of Alauddin Khalji, while the price of a handsome young slave was twenty to thirty *tankahs* and that of a slave-servant ten to fifteen *tankahs*, the price of a child slave-boy *(ghulām bachchagān naukāri)* was seventy to eighty *tankahs*. As these prices were fixed by the Sultan himself, the importance attached by this warlord to young slaves is self-evident.

Alauddin Khalji possessed 50,000 slave-boys, whom he employed on many kinds of duties.[13] Muhammad Tughlaq too

---

11 Ira Marvin Lapidus, *Muslim Cities in the Later Middle Ages*, p. 6, also p. 44.

12 Lal, 'The Ghaznavids in India', *Bengal Past and Present*, Sir Jadunath Sarkar Birth Centenary Number, July-Dec. 1970, pp. 131-152.

13 Barani, pp. 58-59, 314; Afif, pp. 267-72. For details Lal, *Muslim Slave System in Medieval India*, pp. 41-59. The tradition of employing children as artisans and labourers dates from the medieval times. Slave-boys were made to work in manufacturing articles in royal *karkhanas* and private manufactories.

obtained slaves in campaigns. Firoz Tughlaq's acquisition of slaves was accomplished through various ways — capture in war, in lieu of revenue, and presents from nobles. He had instructed his amils and Jagirdars to obtain slave-boys in place of revenue and tribute. This was the position from the Muslim imperialist point of view. The armymen captured slaves — men, women and children — in hundreds and thousands, especially the more vulnerable women and children. But those who were attacked did not submit without resistance. They burnt their women in *jauhar* and many Rajputs, aware of the fate of captured boys, burned the young boys also along with the women. Still others just escaped into inaccessible places with whatever of their property they could carry, and swelled the numbers of SCs/STs and OBCs.

All the same, the numbers of slaves captured by Muslims was large. As the male slaves grew in age, they made the army of the Sultanate strong. They were made Muslims before long and developed all special traits of Muslims as antagonistic to their ancestral religion. Writing both as a theoretician as well as an experienced commentator on the Sultanate's slave system, Ziyauddin Barani says this about the slave-soldiers' loyalty, devotion to duty and courage: "They strive with their hearts and souls for the success of every enterprise. They hurl themselves like balls into running waters and flaming fires. Then it becomes necessary for the whole army (in emulation) to take the same path as they have done. The value of slaves (as a shock-battalion) is obvious."[14] In short, the medieval Muslim slave-system was a constant supplier of loyal troops to the army of the Sultanate.

Another source of strength of this army was the constant inflow of foreign soldiers from Muslim homelands beyond the Indus. These may be called, for the sake of brevity, by the generic terms Turks and Afghans. The Turks came as invaders and became

---

In modern times of Human Rights, efforts are being made to rescue child labourers from their old occupations. Still, they continue to be employed in industries owned mainly by Muslims as per tradition handed down from the Muslim period to our own times — carpet making, bangle-making, yarn-weaving, manufacturing metal utensils, lock-making, fireworks etc.

14 Barani, *Fatawa-i-Jahandari*, p. 25.

rulers, army officers and armymen. The warlike character of the Afghans attracted the notice of conquerors of India who freely enrolled them in their armies. Muhammad Ghauri in his expedition brought ten thousand Afghan horsemen with him.[15] Indian sultans continued the tradition. They had a preference for homeland troops, or any Muslim warriors from the trans-Indus region. In the time of Iltutmish, Jalaluddin of Khawarizm, fleeing before Chingiz Khan, brought contingents of Afghan soldiers with him. In course of time, many of them took service under Iltutmish.[16] Balban employed three thousand Afghan horse and foot in his campaigns against the Mewatis;[17] and appointed thousands of Afghan officers and men for garrisoning forts of Gopalgir, (S.W. of Delhi, near Jaipur), Kampil (in District Farrukhabad U.P.) Patiali (Etah District), Bhojpur (in District Farukkhabad), and Jalali (11 miles east of Aligarh).[18] In the royal processions, hundreds of Sistani, Ghauri, Samarqandi and Arab soldiers with swords drawn, used to march by Balban's side. This indicates constant influx of foreign troops into India.

The Afghans had got accustomed to the adventure of soldiering in India. They joined in large numbers the armies of Mongol invaders as well as of Amir Timur when the latter marched into India in 1398. Like the Afghans, the Mongol (ethnically a generic term, again) soldiers too were there in the army of the Sultanate in large numbers. Jalaluddin Khalji (1290-96) came to terms with a Mongol invading chief and many of the latter's followers joined service of the Sultan. Under Alauddin Khalji, they were called neo-Muslims. Persian element in the rank of officers and men was also prominent. Abyssinian slave-soldiers and officers became prominent under Raziyah.[19] The immigration of

---

15 Niamatullah, *Makhzan-i-Afghana,* N.B. Roy's trs., p.11.

16 Olaf Caroe, *The Pathans,* p. 135.

17 Minhaj, *Tabqat-i-Nasiri,* Text, p. 315.

18 Barani, pp. 57-58.

19 In later times they were obtained mostly (?) through the sea route. In the war between Humayun and Bahadur Shah of Gujarat (1533), the latter entered into a treaty with the Europeans (Portuguese) of Surat, and having through their assistance raised a force of 6,000 Abyssinians returned to Ahmedabad (Jauhar, *Tazkirat al-Waqiat* trs. by C. Stewart, p. 7).

foreign troops continued without break in the time of the Tughlaqs, Saiyyads and Lodis. Under the Saiyyad and Lodi rulers, Afghans of all tribes and clans were invited into Hindustan with high promises, and they flocked into India like 'ants and locusts'. In short, constant induction of foreign soldiers from Muslim lands, contributed to the strength and superiority of the army of the Sultanate.

Indians too were freely enrolled. Ziyauddin Barani was against the recruitment of non-Muslims in the army, but Indian element was prominent in the army of the Sultanate which, according to Al Umri, "consisted of Turks, inhabitants of Khata, Persians, and Indians".[20] Right from the days of Mahmud of Ghazni, Hindus used to join Muslim armies, and lend strength to it.[21]

Most of the Hindus in the Muslim army belonged to the infantry wing and were called Paiks. But all Paiks did not remain Hindus; they were converted to Islam. Paiks, therefore, may be rightly termed as urban infantry. Some of these were poor persons and joined the army for the sake of securing employment. Others were slaves and war-captives. The Paiks cleared the jungles and prepared roads for the army on march. The captives were sometimes used as "cannon fodder" in battle.[22] But others, especially professionals, joined the permanent cadre of infantry for combat purpose. Barbosa (early sixteenth century) says this about them: "They carry swords and daggers, bows and arrows. They are right good archers and their bows are long like those of England. They are mostly Hindus."[23] Many famous Paiks hailed

---

20 Barani, *Fatawa-i-Jahandari*, pp. 25-26; Al Umri, *Masalik-ul-Absar*, E, D, III, p. 576.

21 Utbi, *Kitab-i-Yamini* trs. by Reynolds, pp. 335-336; Farishtah, op, cit., I, p. 18; Bosworth, op. cit., p. 107. Also article on the Ghaznavids by Longworth Dames in the *Encyclopaedia of Islam.*

22 The infantrymen were so placed as to bear the first brunt of the enemy's attack. Consequently, the temptation to flee was great. But they could not leave their posts, for on the field of battle "horses are on their right and left...and behind (them) the elephants so that not one of them can run away" (Al-Qalqashindi, *Subh-i-Asha*, trs. Otto Spies, p. 76).

23 *The Book of Duarte Barbosa,* I, p. 181. It may be noted that when Prince Alauddin Khalji marched against Devagiri, he had with him about 2,000 Paiks (Barani, p. 222).

from Bengal. Their most important weapon was Dhanuk or Dhanush (about the efficacy of which we shall discuss in the Section on weapons). They were renowned for their loyalty. Alauddin Khalji, Mubarak Khalji and Firoz Tughlaq were saved by Paiks when attacked.[24]

Then there were mercenaries or volunteers enrolled on the eve of a campaign. The volunteer element in the army was known by the name of Ghazi. The Ghazis were not entitled to any salary, but relied mostly on "rich pickings from the Indian campaigns". The victories of the Ghaznavids had attracted these plundering adventurers to their standards. The Ghaznavid tradition of enrolling Ghazi mercenaries was continued by the Turkish sultans in India.[25] Writing early in the reign of Iltutmish, Fakhre Mudabbir describes a military review and mentions a body of infantry "who have voluntarily joined the forces".[26] On his way to Lakhnauti, Balban enrolled about 2,00,000 horsemen and infantry. Raziyah, when she marched with her husband Altuniah to re-capture the throne, is reported to have headed an army composed mainly of mercenaries from the Khokhar and Jat tribes of the Punjab. Right up to the Tughlaq times and beyond, mercenaries (Muslims, says Afif for Firoz's times) joined the army for love of plunder and concomitant gains. Unrestricted plunder of infidels by Muslim soldiers was allowed by Islamic law. The state took one-fifth of the loot as its own share called *Khums*. Such incentives added enthusiasm and strength to the regular army.

Enrolment in the regular cadre depended on a number of considerations like personal prowess, skill in weapons and family background. The times believed in the theory of 'martial class'. Fakhre Mudabbir advises that those whose ancestors had not been soliders should not be made officers, Sawars or

---

24 Barani, p. 593, also 52, 273, 376, 377.

25 E.g. Minhaj, *Tabqat-i-Nasiri,* Text, p. 317; Barani, p. 80; Afif, p. 289.

26 Fakhr-i-Mudabbir, *Adab-ul-Harb wa Shujaat*, Hindi trs. by S.A.A Rizvi in *Adi Turk Kalin Bharat,* fol. 109 b.

Sarkhails.[27] Ziyauddin Barani also expresses similar views.[28] However, recruitment seems to have been based on merit, and troops were enrolled after a hard and gruelling test. Describing the scene of the review and fresh enrolment before the Governor of Multan, which was an important centre of recruitment throughout the Sultanate period, Ibn Battuta says: "This Amir was sitting on a big dais.... Near him was the Qazi and the Khatib. On his right and left were military chiefs; the armed warriors stood high behind his head. The troops passed before him in review. There were many bows. When anyone came desiring to enlist as an archer in the army, he was given one of these bows to pull.... And if he desired to be enlisted in the cavalry a drum was placed. He would drive his horse and strike it with his lance. A ring was also suspended against a small wall. The horseman would make his horse run until he came abreast of it. Should he succeed in lifting it up with his lance he was considered an excellent horseman. If one desired to enlist as a mounted archer, a ball was placed on the ground. The candidate galloped on horseback and aimed the arrow at the ball. His salary was fixed proportionately to his success in striking the ball."[29] The learned and experienced chronicler of the Sultanate period, Maulana Ziyauddin Barani, realised the importance of recruitment after a thorough test and says, "The *ghazis* and *mujahids* (holy warriors) should be tested in the art of horsemanship, so that other people, who have nothing to do with the art of war and belong to groups of artisans and other professions, do not find a place among them. The enrolment of amateurs among veterans throws the work of the army into disorder. To secure the increase and stability of the army, the officers ought to be select and distinguished men, well-born, brave and virtuous."[30] In brief, the recruitment of troops was based on merit which was determined

27 *Adab-ul-Harb*, fol. 49 a.

28 Barani, *Fatawa-i-Jahandari,* p.2.

29 Ibn Battuta, p. 14.

30 Barani, *Fatawa-i-Jahandari*, p. 25.

after a severe test.[31]

Like the procedure of recruitment, the process of training too was hard. If the Samanid traditions had not been given up in India, the training of a slave-soldier described in Nizam-ul-Mulk's *Siyasat Nama* should have turned him into a veteran warrior in the course of a few years. In the first year after his purchase, the *ghulam* was trained as a foot-solider, and was never permitted, under penalties, to mount a horse. In his second year, he was given a horse with plain saddle. After another year's training he received an ornamental belt, and so on. By the seventh year alone was he fully trained and fit to become a tent-commander.[32] The training of a boy-slave recruit in the Sultanate might have been more or less similar. Details about such training are not available in medieval Muslim chronicles, but Barani does hint at it when he speaks about Balban's trained soldiers (*tarbiyat-yāfta lashkar)*.[33] Kafur Hazardinari was trained in the capital and at court for ten years (1299-1308) before he was sent as commander of the expedition to the South. For experienced soldiers, enrolled in the fashion described by Ibn Battuta, constant campaigns, tournaments, sport, shikar and regular reviews were enough to keep them fit and alert.[34]

The Mounts

The Sultanate's army comprised both cavalry and infantry. It had an elephant corps. Camels and ponies and other animals were also used for commissariat service. But the most important wing of the army which gave it immense power of punch was the cavalry.

Cavalry comprises the man and his mount. We have discussed the prowess of men; we shall now turn to the study of the Sultanate's horses. In India, only in some places of eastern Punjab like the Shiwaliks, Samana, Sunnam, Tabarhind, Thanesar and the

31 Barani, p. 102.
32 Ruben Levy, *The Social Structure of Islam* p. 74.
33 Barani, pp. 51-52.
34 Minhaj, p. 225; Al Qalqashindi, p. 75; Afif, pp. 317, 322.

'Country of the Khokhars', good quality horses were found in sufficient numbers.[35] But these horses were inferior to the horse of West-Asia breed, and importation of war-horses from abroad became an imperative necessity for the sultans of Delhi. Good quality war-horses were responsible in good measure for the victory of the Ghaznavids and Ghaurids in northern India.[36] But after the initial establishment of Muslim power, the supply of war-horses occasionally got disrupted. The Khokhar region was in an imperfect state of subjugation. Roads were infested with recalcitrant elements and Mongol marauders, and Balban had to undertake stern measures to clear the roads for caravans[37] in order to obtain horses.

Medieval chroniclers speak of Yamani, Shami, Bahri and Qipchagi horses as being in use by soliders in India, and there was largescale importation of horses into India from Arabia, Persia, Afghanistan and even the steppe lands of southern Russia, known as Tatars. This trade yielded so much profit that in peace time it was not normally cut off even by the Chaghatai Khans of Transoxiana or their deputies.[38] Thus apart from regular traders, even Mongol raiders and tribal groups sometimes sold horses for the Delhi army. Ibn Battuta, after describing his journey through the Crimea and his arrival at Azof writes: "The horses in the country are exceedingly numerous and their price is negligible...These horses are exported to India (in droves) each one numbering six thousand more or less... When they reach the land of Sind with their horses, they feed them with forage, because the vegetation of the land of Sindh does not take the place of barley and the greater part of the horses die or are stolen. They are taxed on them seven silver dinars a horse and pay a further tax at Multan, the capital of the land of Sindh. In spite of this, there remains a handsome profit for the traders in these horses.

35 Barani, p. 53.

36 Lal, 'The Ghaznavids in India', op.cit., pp. 131-152, esp. p.137

37 Barani, *Fatawa-i-Jahandari*, pp. 57-58.

38 Simon Digby, *War Horse and Elephant in the Delhi Sultanate*, p. 34; Barani, pp. 461-62; Lal, *Twilight*, pp. 131, 329.

The good horses are worth 500 (silver) dinars or more.[39]

Besides making direct purchases from abroad, the sultans of Delhi also replenished their *paigahs* with horses of foreign breed obtained from defeated Indian princes, particularly those with access to the sea as they imported such horses in large numbers. The South and Gujarat provided war-horses in particular, and the Deccan expeditions of Malik Kafur were most successful in this respect. For example, Raja Pratap Rudradeva of Warangal, making peace with Malik Kafur in 709 A.H. (1310 CE), is said to have surrendered 20,000 Kohi and Bahri horses. On Malik Kafur's final Deccan expedition an unspecified number of horses was surrendered by the Hoysala ruler. In the plunder of the stables of the Pandya Raja, 5,000 fine horses of the Yamini, Shami and Bahri breed had been taken. Annual tribute of such imported horses were also imposed upon the Hindu rulers of the Deccan. In 717 A.H., the Warangal king was required by Mubarak Shah Khalji to remit annually to Delhi 1,000 horses as well as 100 elephants.[40]

According to Ziyauddin Barani. Alauddin Khalji is said to have had 70,000 horses in his stables or *paigahs* (in Delhi).[41] The Arab geographer Ahmad Abbas Al Umri states that Sultan Muhammed Tughlaq distributed to his retinue 10,000 Arab horses and countless others. Even Firoz Tughlaq, who is said to have neglected the army, maintained extensive *paigahs*.[42] In the later fourteenth century the royal *paigahs* had become so large that these were distributed between five establishments. One of these was situated within the palace at the capital, and the other four were all at some distances from Delhi.[43] Horses, however, were

---

39 Simon Digby, op. cit., pp. 35-36 quoting from Ibn Battuta, French ed., II, pp. 371-74 and Gibb's trs., II (Cambridge, 1958-59), pp. 478-79.

40 Amir Khusrau, *Khazain-ul-Futuh* ed. M.W. Mirza, (Calcutta, 1953), p. 101, English trs. by M.Habib entitled *Campaigns of Alauddin Khilji* (Madras, 1931), p. 72. Also *Nuh Sipihr*, ed. Wahid Mizra (O.U.P., Calcutta, 1948), p. 128; *Khazain-ul-Futuh*, pp. 138, 163.

41 Barani, p. 262.

42 Afif, pp. 339-340.

43 Ibid., pp. 318, 340.

a 'perishable' commodity, and deaths and even epidemics among them were common.[44] Therefore, foreign-breed war-horses were constantly imported to keep the *paigahs* well stocked.

These horses and the predominant place of cavalry in the army of the Sultanate gave it an advantage over that of the Hindus. Balban believed that with six or seven thousand horse he could lay waste the territories of Hindu rulers who possessed a hundred thousand foot soldiers.[45] Individual Hindu king's cavalry could not be as large as that of the central Delhi Sultanate.[46] An idea of the cavalry of the Sultanate can be had from the fact that when Kaiqubad made preparations to march against his father, Nasiruddin Bughra Khan of Bengal, he mustered 100,000 soldiers at Delhi.[47] Alauddin Khalji had under his command 475,000 horsemen,[48] and Muhammad Tughlaq's cavalry is said to have consisted of 900,000 soldiers.[49] Of course, the size of the army varied from time to time. The Saiyyads were weak and Lodis not so strong. But even in the newly formed kingdoms of the fifteenth century like Gujarat, Malwa, Jaunpur etc., Muslim cavalry generally had an edge over the armies of the neighbouring Rajas.

Hindus also imported foreign-breed horses. Since the ancient times the balance of trade was in India's favour, and India obtained precious metals in large quantities. But the one commodity for importing which Indian kings paid the foreigners in gold was war-horses. About Malabar, which was situated far away from northern India, but was connected with West Asia by sea, Marco Polo says that there no horses were bred and "thus a great part of the wealth of the country is wasted on purchasing horses" brought by merchants of Kis and Hormuz and Aden.[50] Abdulla

44 Yazdi, *Zafar Namah*, II, pp. 59-70.

45 Barani, p. 52.

46 Minhaj, pp. 215-16; Afif, 119.

47 Amir Khusrau, *Qiran-us-Sadain*, pp. 35, 47.

48 Farishtah, I, p. 200.

49 Ahmad Abbas, *Masalik-ul-Absar*, E. D., III, p. 576; Al-Qalqashindi, *Subh-ul-Asha*, p. 66.

50 Henry Yule, *Ser Marco Polo*, II, p. 340.

Wassaf says that Indians did not even give these precious mounts a proper diet, and they were fed on "dressed gram and milk". Once in a while they were taken out for ceremorial and festive parades and made to run fast. Improper diet, undue rest and then sudden exertion killed many horses. In this way large numbers used to die every year and new ones were imported. Wassaf further says that in this way 10,000 horses were imported annually into Mabar, Kambayat and other western Indian ports and 2,200,000 dinars (220 of red gold for each) were paid for them.[51] The Indian kings also bore the cost of all the horses lost during the voyage.

This is the evidence with regard to western and southern India. About the north, where rulers continually encountered the Muslim invaders, little is known. It may be presumed that they obtained war-horses from the Shiwaliks and the country of the Khokhars. These regions were not entirely subdued by Muslim rulers and were mostly unconverted to Islam. But their horses were of inferior quality and not plentiful in supply. Therefore, the cavalry wing of Rajputs was not as strong as that of the Muslims. This fact may be the cause and effect of a phenomenon observed in medieval Hindu forts. From the construction technique of these citadels it appears that their armies were not cavalry-oriented. It would even seem probable that infantry was regarded more important while cavalry was neglected. One thing is clear: horses could not be stationed in large numbers in the forts constructed on hill tops, and medieval Hindu forts were almost invariably built on the top of hillocks. This is apparent on an examination of the forts of Devagiri, Asirgath, Champanir and Raisen, which I have personally visited and studied in some detail.

The citadel of Devagiri is situated on an isolated cone-shaped hill 640 feet high from the ground. The rock is steep, and a moat is cut into the solid rock 50 feet deep perpendicular. There can be no question that Devagiri, both in design and construction,

---

51 Wassaf, p. 302.

was one of the strongest forts of early medieval India,[52] and yet there is no path by which horses could go up and be stationed in it. There is a subterranean passage, leading to the top of the hill and into the fort, but it has stairs for ascent, precluding climbing of the horses. Asirgarh too is situated on a very high hill and but for the graduated-gradient roads built by Akbar and developed since then, stationing of horses inside the fortress should have been impossible. Raisen, even with modern approach roads and beaten tracks, would not permit ascent of horses. Similar is the case with Champanir.

It appears that in the early medieval period the main wing of the army of Hindu Rajas was only infantry. The elephants were used by the important persons for riding in the battle-field and these together with horses were probably kept at the base of the hillock on which the fort stood. This was strategically unwise as the invader at the first opportunity, captured the mounts at the time of investment of the citadel.[53] It has been mentioned above that Pratap Rudradeva of Warangal "surrendered" to Malik Kafur 20,000 horses,[54] and 5,000 fine horses were taken in plunder from the stables of the Pandya ruler. And there is no reason to disbelieve Amir Khusrau, Barani and Farishtah. Would it not follow that most of these mounts were kept in stables at the foot of the fort? On the other hand, the sultans of Delhi, from the very beginning of their rule, built fortresses on ground level, or almost on ground level, like Siri, Kilughari, Tughlaqabad, Kotla Firoz Shah, at Mandu and in Gujarat — not to speak of Mughal forts of Agra, Delhi and Allahabad — for efficient deployment of cavalry. When Muhammad Tughlaq developed Daulatabad (Devagiri), he built new fort walls and bastions starting at the ground level.

It would be a bold statement to make, but in the medieval period Hindu rulers gave importance mainly to infantry and

52 Sidney Toy, *The Strongholds of India*, p. 33.
53 Barani, p. 223; Farishtah, p. 95.
54 Ibid., p. 330 has 7,000.

elephants, and the cavalry wing was developed only in course of time.[55] On the other hand, cavalry was the main branch and the best source of strength of the army of Muslim invaders and their descendants, the Turkish Sultans of India. It was but natural that in the regions of Central and West Asia, where good quality horses were found, their accoutrement and equipment — stirrup, horse-shoe and saddle — should have been invented and developed. In India, in the paintings of Ajanta all horsemen are without stirrups. While some eleventh century bronze stirrups used by Ghaznavids are preserved in the Museums of Kabul and Ghazni, P.K. Gode affirms that there is nothing to show that the Rajputs used them in pre-Muslim times.[56] The evidence regarding the shoeing of horses and the military advantage of this in Indian conditions of the time is not available. Horse-shoe may have been in use in India, but it is not seen in paintings and sculptures fixed as it is at the bottom of the hoof.

However, the use of saddles by the Hindus cannot be denied. But the use of metal stirrups by a heavily caparisoned cavalier added to his advantage. The rider was seated firmly on the saddle with both feet stuck fast in the stirrups leaving both the hands free for wielding lances and bows, and shooting long arrows from the horse-back. This made the Ghaznavid and Ghaurid

---

55 Some equestrian statues have been discovered at Gool village, 210 kilometers north of Jammu. These are important as they depict the elaborate harness of the horses and robes and armour of the cavaliers. They clearly show that cavalry was in vogue in the Kashmir Valley in the medieval times. But we are not sure about the date of the statues. Vidya Ratan Khajuria, former Curator of the Dogra Art Gallery of Jammu, places these in the pre-Muslim period and says that they are not less than 700 years old. On the other hand, K. N. Shastri, former Excavation Assistant of the Archaeological Survey of India, thinks that they belong to the period of Maharaja Gulabsingh (1792-1857). Gool is located at an altitude of 2100 meters in the mountain recesses, but is connected through a 50-km. road with the Jammu-Srinagar highway. The find is interesting, but there is nothing surprising about the use of horses for war pruposes in Kashmir and north-west Punjab. Horses were always available in these regions. However, these statues do not prove that cavalry was an important wing of Rajput armies throughout northern India in the Sultanate period. For detalis see *The Times of India,* 5th July, 1977.

56 P. K. Gode, *Studies in Indian Cultural History* , II, p. 76.

horsemen formidable in the battlefield. This tradition was inherited by the horse-soldiers of the Sultanate. It is indicated by the likeness of horsemen engraved on the coins of earlier sultans like Iltutmish, "where the horse is seen at full charge, and the rider with upraised mace, the special weapon of the great Mahmud. The form of the saddle, the seat of the horseman, the *chanfrein* or head-armour of the steed, all seem to point to *Turki* ideals."[57]

As against the cavalry of the sultans, the Indian rulers depended for military strength on elephants. But even in this sphere the sultans became predominant in a short time. For, they obtained for their *pīlkhānā* elephants from all possible sources, in plunder, in tribute from subordinate rulers or provincial governors, by purchasing from outside Muslim-ruled territories, or by trapping them directly from the forest regions. There is, and will always be, a controversy about the real efficacy of the elephant in medieval warfare. It is on record that on many occasions Rajput princes lost in war because, at a crucial moment, the elephant they were riding, ran away from the field of battle, wounded or enraged. Mongol raiders continually attacked India in spite of the Delhi sultans deploying elephants against them. Nothing could be achieved by Nasiruddin Mahmud Tughlaq, Ibrahim Lodi and Rana Sanga against Timur and Babur, although the former had huge war elephants. During the post-Aurangzeb period, when the use of cannons and large guns had become common, neither the Mughals nor the Marathas could check the onrush of foreign invaders in spite of their elephant

---

57 Edward Thomas, *The Chronicles of the Pathan Kings of Delhi*, pp. 78-79. Alberuni makes a very interesting statement which gives a point of vantage to the cavalrymen from abroad. Writing about "the strange habits of the Hindus", he says, "They ride without a saddle, but if they put on a saddle, they mount the horse from its right side...They fasten the *kuthāra* (i.e. the dagger) at the waist on the right side" (*Alberuni's India*, I, p. 181).

If the Hindus mounted the horse from the right side, they must have swung their left leg to do so. In that case any weapon worn on the left side would have obstructed the process of mounting and naturally, as asserted by Alberuni, they wore the dagger or the sword on the right side. This could not have been drawn out of the scabbard with as much agility and ease with the right hand as any weapon worn on the left side. If true, this was definitely disadvatageous.

corps.[58]

But in the Sultanate period the elephant occupied an important place in warfare. Heavily armoured, it could be used as a living battering ram for pulling down the gates of a fortress. Many of the strongest forts in India have elephant spikes upon their doors to prevent such form of assault. The elephant could also serve as a pack animal carrying a very large load. Its gigantic size created a feeling of terror in the enemy ranks. War elephants could kill and destroy systematically.[59] Naturally, the Sultans of Delhi tried to acquire as many elephants as they could. Mahmud of Ghazni had taken hundreds of them from India. According to Minhaj Siraj he had 2,500 of them; a *pīlkhānā* of his in Ghazni could accommodate 1,000 elephants.[60] Balban thought about them with wistful emotion and considered one elephant equal to 500 war-horses. However, the Elephant Corps in the Sultanate until the time of Balban could not have been large, but he and succeeding Muslim monarchs were very keen to obtain elephants from wherever they could. In fact, when Balban established Bughra Khan in Bengal, he laid it down as a condition that war-horses would not be sent to Bengal until Bughra Khan regularly sent elephants to Delhi.[61] Alauddin Khalji got the largest number of elephants from the South.[62] Most of the elephants came from Bengal which was an area where war elephants were trapped locally. Firoz Tughlaq obtained elephants

58 Nadir Shah is said to have remarked: "What strange practice is this the rulers of Hind have adopted? In the day of the battle they ride on an elephant and make themselves into a target for every body?" (Rao Dalpat Singh, *Malahat-i-Maqal* cited by W. Irvine in *The Army of the Indian Moghuls*, London, 1903, p. 177).

Irvine adds: "Long before the Moghul empire fell into decay, they (the elephants) had become principally beasts of burden or means of display, and their role in the day of battle was comparatively insignificant" (Ibid., p. 176).

59 Barbosa, I, p. 118.

60 *Tabqat-i-Nasiri*, Text, p. 10; trs., I., p. 83.

61 Barani, p. 53.

62 In 1308-9, 17 elephants were taken by Kafur in his sack of Devagiri (Barani, p. 326). Next year he got 100 elephants from the Rai of Warangal (*Khazain-ul-Futuh*, p. 101). In the campaign of 1310-12, the total number captured was 512 to 612 (Barani, p. 333; *Khazain*, p. 161).

from Bengal, and hunted and captured many in Orissa. He acquired Ceylon elephants (from *jazair* islands) also, and compensated the (Gujarat) traders for the animals killed in transit.[63] South India and Gujarat also imported elephants from Ceylon.

However, the strength of the Elephant Corps in the Delhi Sultanate even in its heyday does not seem to be great. Al Umri says that there were 3000 elephants in the *pīlkhānā* of Muhammad bin Tughlaq, but according to Simon Digby, a "maximum number from 750 to 1,000 war elephants in the possession of the Delhi Sultans in the period of their greatest power in the early 14th century appears not unlikely".[64] In such a situation the claim of Barani that the sultans of Delhi had the monopoly of the elephants[65] is not correct.[66] It would only be correct to presume that the Delhi sultans possessed larger number of war elephants than their own provincial governors or independent Rajput rulers. This provided the army of the Sultanate added strength. At the battle of Kili (1299), Alauddin put many elephants in the field, and the Mongols are said to have been defeated because of this.[67] Timur's army was scared to fight against the army of Nasiruddin Mahmud as the latter had huge war-elephants.[68]

Weapons

We may now turn to discuss the superiority (or otherwise) of the weapons of the army of the Sultanate. As has been pointed out earlier its most important element was heavy cavalry. It was armed with the bow and arrows for engaging in combat from a distance and with one or more weapons for hand to hand fighting — the lance, the short spear, the mace, the lasso. The most commonly employed weapon of close combat was the sword.

63 Afif, pp. 163, 167 ff., 486.

64 Digby, op.cit. p. 59.

65 Barani, p. 594.

66 Sultan Mahmud Sharqi of Jaunpur marched against Delhi (1452) with a thousand elephants (Farishtah, I, p. 157; II, p. 308; Lal, *Twilight*, p. 135).

67 Isami, *Futuh-us-Salatin*, p. 260.

68 Lal, *Twilight*, pp. 23-24.

Fakhr-i-Mudabbir gives clear primacy to the bow, the most effective of the weapons of the horseman, and next he emphasises the superiority of the sword. Of the regional varieties of the bow in use, Fakhr-i-Mudabbir first mentions the Chachi (named after Chach or Shash, modern Tashkend) and the Khwarazmi, in use among the people of Transoxiana. He then commends to archers the bows of Ghazna and Lahore and of two proximate geographical areas. He mentions next the mountain bow found in certain foothills (probably Salt Range and the foothills of the Punjab Himalayas). These mountain bows were made wholly of horn and they were true in their aim. The last variety of bow which is mentioned is the Indian bow *(kamān-i-hindavi)*. It is these with which the Rajput armies faced the Muslim invaders and the armies of the Sultanate were mainly equipped. It was made from cane (*nay, neza* of male bamboo?), and its bowstring was also made from the bark of cane. Its arrows did not travel very far, but at a shorter distance it inflicted a very bad wound. Most of such arrow-heads were poisoned. The conclusion to be drawn from this information is that the bows generally in use in the late Ghazvnavid and Ghaurid army, in addition to being considered superior to those in use in Central Asia, had a longer range than the bows mainly used by the Rajput opponents in northern India, but were not a decisively superior weapon to these. However, three types of archer's thumb-rings are mentioned by Fakhr-i-Mudabbir, all with clearly Muslim names. It is, therefore, possible that the thumb-ring may not at this time had been in use among the Rajputs.

If Fakhr-i-Mudabbir's evidence regarding the bows is indecisive, he is quite clear that the Indians had superior techniques or materials for the manufacture of the sword. He makes mention about many famous varieties of swords,[69] but among them all the Hindi sword is the best and most lustrous *(gawhardaratar)*. His preference for Indian swords is not surprising. Many references

69 *Adab-ul-Harab*, p. 69. Also Rizvi, *Uttat Timur Kalin Bharat*, Aligarh, 1958, p, 177.

show the esteem in which they were held throughout the medieval Islamic world. Their export to such distant areas as Umayyad Spain and Seljuq Anatolia is attested. Fakhr-i-Mudabbir mentions several varieties of the Hindi sword. "These blades are cherished by all the Ranas, Thakurs and men of the tribes (*mardum-i-qabail)* and they are very sharp for wounding." By this last piece of information, Fakhr-i-Mudabbir makes clear that the best of Indian swords were also in the hands of the North Indian Rajput opponents of the Muslim armies. He also declares that there is no better lance than the Indian[70] His evidence appears decisive in concluding that the Muslim conquest and ascendancy was not based on a technological superiority in weapons of close combat.[71]

But as resources of the Ghaznavids and Ghaurids were superior to those of Hindu rulers of the Punjab,[72] Muslim sultans in India had better resources than the Rajputs. They had in their possession Punjab and Sind and the fertile Ganga-Yamuna Doab from the very beginning. With their superior resources, the Turks had developed a magnificent strategy of war, which had come down to Indian sultans as a legacy from Central Asia. Fakhr-i-Mudabbir points out that the Turko-Persian principles and methods of campaigns, encampments and strategy were superior to those of the Hindus.[73] His detailed study of fighting patrols, proper seasons and times of attack, tactics of ambuscade, selection of the battlefield, arrangements of rank and file, protection of standard bearers, distribution of loot in war, etc., gives the clue to the success of the Muslim army. It gained constantly in experience by coming into conflict (and contact) with the foreign Mongol invaders.[74]

---

70 *Adab-ul-Harb*, 107a.

71 The above two paragraphs are based mainly on Mudabbir's *Adab-ul-Harb* as ably analysed by Simon Digby, op.cit., pp. 15-20.

72 Lal, 'The Ghaznavids in India', op.cit., pp. 131-152.

73 *Adab-ul-Harb*, fol. 112.

74 The Mongols "understood the art of feigning reatreat, of envelopment and of surprise, and, as battle after battle was fought against nations employing different methods of warfare, the sum of their experience had made them invincible" (Sykes, *A History of Persia*, II, p. 85).

The sultans of Delhi had to repeatedly encounter the descendants of such warriors and used to gain new experience in warfare.

Its use of the engines of war[75] like *arrada, gargach, minjniq, maghrabi, haqqaha* (rockets) etc., the mobility of its cavalry, and the expertise of archers had made it very powerful.[76] Moreover, from the time of Iltutmish to that of Firoz Shah great development had taken place both in the field of strategy and manufacture of weapons and engines of war. Alauddin Khalji's deployment of engines of war helped in the conquest of a major part of the India. The *Sirat-i-Firoz Shahi* mentions some very interesting "equipments, outfits and instruments for waging war". These were kept stored in the royal *kārkhānas* and included traps, nets, noose and snare. In the midst of a hotch-potch of assortment of items "we find a brief reference to such instruments as...Bandiqa (venetian cross-bow for throwing stone balls); Faraqha Falakhun (slings made of rope for throwing stones); Kaman Guruha (large mounted cross bow); Harf-i-Kilk (arrow with inverted harp points); Julahiq (balls of stone thrown by ballists); Zand-i-Atash (incendiary fire-steel) etc".[77] In view of the fact that evidence regarding the use of similar engines and weapons by the Rajputs is conspicuous by its absence, their use by the army of the Sultanate assigns to it a superior position.

Weapons, equipments, engines, instruments etc. for waging war are mentioned not only in the *Sirat-i- Firoz Shahi*. There are manuals in the Persian language written right from the tenth century onwards dealing elaborately with the art of warfare. These would have provided guidance to the sultans in India on military matters. The *Qabus Nama,* for instance, written by Kaikaus in the year 475 A.H. (1082-83 CE), has three chapters on "On Buying Horses", "On Giving Battle to the Enemy" and on "The Art of Controlling an Armed Force". Similarly, Nizam-ul-Mulk's *Siyasat Nama* written in 485 A.H. (1092-93 CE) contains two short chapters on "Having Troops of Various Races"

---

75 *Adab-ul-Harb* has detailed notices in fols. 115-156.

76 Lal, *Khaljis*, 192-93.

77 S.M. Ashari, 'A study of the rare Ms. Sirat-i-Firoz Shahi', *Journal of Indian History*, Vol. LII, April 1947, Pt. I, pp. 127-146, esp. p. 139.

and "On Preparting Arms and Equipment for War Expeditions".[78]

These are not very detailed works. But *Adab-ul-Harb wa Shujaat* of Fakir-i-Muddabir, written in India around 1206 CE, is an excellent treatise on administration in general and on military matters in particular. It contains chapters like "Counsel regarding war" (chapter 7), "Horses, their peculiar features and their good and bad points" (chapters 8, 9, 10), "Use of weapons" (11), "Recruitment of soldiers and review of the army" (12, 13), "Fighting patrols and night attack" (14, 15). All the chapters right up to 34 deal with the theory and practice of war.[79] *Adab-ul-Harb* itself was succeeded by a number of similar treaties like Ziyauddin Barani's *Fatawa-i-Jahandari,* Firoz Tughlaq's *Sirat-i-Firozshahi* and *Tuzuk-i-Timuri* (translated as *Institutes of Timur* by Davy). In this regard the Yesa of Chingiz too would have given guidance to the sultans in warfare.

The Rajputs were lagging much behind the Turks in this sphere. They had hardly any works on military science with the result that one has to reconstruct the chief features of their art of war with the help of casual references, accounts of actual or mythical wars contained in the contemporary Hindu literature or inscriptions, or gleaned from the Muslim sources themselves. For the early medieval period mention of officers like *pilupati* (Elephant Commander), *ashvapati* (Cavalry Commander) etc. is found in Dhanapal's *Tilakmanjari*. The *Lekhapaddhati* (a collection of model inscriptions) mentions forty weapons.[80] Some details of these weapons and other aspects of the Hindu art of war are preserved in *Kānhaḍade-prabandha* of Padmanabh[81] which was composed in V.S. 1512 (1455 CE). Other historical works (and not military manuals) are of dates even later than this. The

78 M. S. Khan, 'The Life & Works of Fakhr-i-Mudabbir', *Islamic Culture,* April 1977, pp. 138-40.

79 *Adab-ul-Harb.*, fols. 66 to 190, Rizvi's trs., pp. 257-272.

80 *Lekhapaddhati*, Geakward Oreiental Series, Baroda, 1925, p. 97.

81 *Rajasthan Through the Ages*, Vol. I, ed. Dasrath Sharma, Rajasthan State Archives, Bikaner, 1966, pp. 710 ff.

availability of so many works on the art of war with the Turks and their lack with the Rajputs helped make the army of the Sultanate a strong military force.

Organisation

In addition to all the factors mentioned above, one very important fact which has ever to be borne in mind is that all medieveal chroniclers and political thinkers give the army a very important place in Islamic polity. Ziyauddin Barani declares: "Kingship is the army and the army kingship,"[82] that is, the main strength and sustenance of the monarch is the army more than anything else. So also say all others. The utmost importance given to the army is best reflected in its efficient upkeep.

The sultan was the supreme commander of the forces, *de jure* as well as *de facto*. He may not have been conversant with the Law, he may have known nothing about revenue matters, he may even have been illiterate, but he had to be a Jihadist, a warrior and a commander. His deficiencies were of little consequence: Al-Qalqashindi mentions that in the field of battle the sultan stood surrounded by the ulema. They could always advise him on how to deal with the *kafir* enemy. For administrative purposes, the army was placed under the charge of the *Diwan-i-Arz* or Minister of War. He was a very important minister, next only to Wazir, and he considered his post as "the guardianship of the empire". Army officers were very highly paid. According to Shihabuddin Al Umri, a Khan received 200,000 *tankahs*, each being worth eight *dirhams* (silver coins). "This sum belongs to him personally, and he is not expected to disburse any part of it to the soldiers... The Maliks received 60 to 50 thousand and an Amir from 40 to 30 thousand *tankahs*."[83] There was no system of budgeting in those days but there is no doubt that major part of the state revenue was expended on the army. If the salary of a soldier was not less than what was paid in Alauddin's days, the

82 *Fatawa-i-Jahandari*, p. 22.
83 *Masalik*, E. D., III, p. 577.

annual salary of Muhammad Tughlaq's 900,000 troops alone would have come to more than 200 million *tankahs*. High salaries to officers and to good soldiers naturally increased the efficiency of the army.

Good salary was not all. Periodical reviews of the army, whether in headquarters or in camp, kept the soldiers on their toes and their mounts in good shape. After Alauddin Khalji had recoganised his army, "soliders from the cities of the empire were tested before the Diwan-i-Arz in archery. Those who were good shots and also possessed good arms were confirmed."[84] The *Diwan-i-Arz* maintained a descriptive roll of every soldier whether in permanent employment or recruited temporarily,[85] and this was the only way of ascertaining his identity in days when there was no photography. Under the Khaljis the system of branding the horse and keeping a written portraiture of the soldier was strictly observed.[86] The system of *dagh wa chihra* (cauterization and descriptive roll) was discontinued by Firoz Tughlaq, but it was revived by Sikandar Lodi and reintroduced by Sher Shah in all elaborateness. It ensured that at the time of review no soldier could send a substitute and no horse could be presented twice, or replaced by an inferior one after the review. However, as good quality horses were costly,[87] and all the soldiers could not always afford to keep high breed horses, many of them greased the palm of the clerks at the *Diwan-i-Arz* to get a fitness certificates. Many others, in spite of repeated reminders, just did not appear for review.[88] Bribery did often succeed,[89] if not under strong rulers.

Barani emphasises the importance of review and says: "It is necessary after examination to prepare a record of the horse and arms of the men twice a year. The soldiers should be examined

84 Barani, p. 319
85 *Adab-ul-Harb*, fol. 107a, 110a; *Masalik*, E. D., III, p. 576.
86 Barani, p.145
87 Al-Qalqashindi, p.47
88 Afif, pp. 299-301.
89 Ibid., p. 57.

by persons concerning whom there can be no suspicion of misappropriation or falsehood, so that there may be no tumult at the time of postings or during battles. This review (*arz*) should be at such times and places that it can be finished at one stretch. The order of review should be for all."[90] The review could be done easily and systematically, for the army was organised on the decimal system. A Sarkhail commanded ten troops, and the hierarchy of officers rose by decimal progression to units commanded by Sarkhail, Sipahsalar, Amir, Malik, to the supreme command of Khan.[91] The review was elaborate and inspection of soldiers minute. According to Amir Khusrau it took fourteen days for the muster roll and inspection of the army that went to Warangal in 1309.[92]

If the demands on the soldier for efficient turn-out were exacting, and if the punishments for desertion and disobedience were severe,[93] he was also very well looked after by the regime. A soldier's salary was fixed according to his merit, efficiency and effectiveness,[94] leaving no ground for grouse. Alauddin Khalji, however, seems to have paid a fixed salary of about 20 *tankahs* a month (234 *tankahs* a year). Although there is no mention of a pay scale or rate of increment, the price freeze of articles of everyday use in his reign was done primarily for the benefit of the armymen.[95] In any case, twenty *tankahs* a month was no small amount. Some slave troops were given (in addition to pay?) free ration and clothing.[96] Many others, captains and

90 *Fatawa-i-Jahandari*, p. 25. Mohammed Habib appends a note saying: "Our authorities often refer to soldiers coming for *arz* or review to Delhi. Standing on the Tughlaqabad fort one can see a space of several square miles enclosed by a crumbling wall. Very possibly this is the spot where the review was held. The review had to be finished at one stretch to prevent the arms, and possibly also the horse, of one trooper being presented again by another."

91 Barani, p. 145; Hajiuddabir, *Zafar-ul-Walih*, p. 782; *Khazain-ul-Futuh*, Habib trs., p. 58.

92 *Khazain-ul-Futuh*, Habib trs., p. 58.

93 Barani, p. 253, Afif, p. 173.

94 Ibn Battuta, p. 17.

95 Barani, pp. 303-304. Also Lal, *Khaljis*, pp. 217-19.

96 *Maslik*, E. D., III, p. 577. Also al-Qalqashindi, p. 71.

soldiers, were assigned land in lieu of pay.[97] The plea of political theorists and the practice of many rulers was to distribute conquered land among Musalmans.[98]

For a soldier an expedition was also an economic venture.[99] Salaries, rewards and emoluments of the army personnel were good.[100] Occasional loot made them still better.[101] During the march and in camp, every care was taken to make the soldier happy.[102] When Ziyauddin Barani recommended that "the *Ariz* (Muster Master) should be kinder to the soldiers than a mother and a father,"[103] he was only reiterating what was actually in practice. Balban's *Ariz* treated the troops kindly and helped deserving men with money.[104] If an officer needed a small loan, it was advanced to him; if his horse got disabled, it was replaced. The advice of Alauddin Khalji to Malik Kafur on the latter's expedition to Warrangal delineates the consideration that was shown to the troops.[105] A number of grocers and merchants used to accompany the army on the march,[106] and friendly kingdoms through which it passed also established markets to cater for its needs.[107] But there were occasions when the hoped for provisions through plunder could not be obtained, and in the absence of a regular commissariat service, the troops suffered badly.[108] Some times, many soldiers unable to bear hardship or disappointed with the quantum of loot, deserted the camp or rebelled.[109] But such occasions were made rare by fear of dire punishments, the

97 Barani, p. 80; Afif, pp. 94-96.
98 *Adab-ul-Harb*, fol. 156 a; Barani, p. 327.
99 Afif, p. 57.
100 Abas Sarwani in Roy's trs. of *Makhzan-i-Afghana*, pp. 67-69; Dorn, p. 44.
101 Farishtah, I. p. 162; Yahiya, p. 188.
102 Afif, pp. 144, 201.
103 *Fatawa-i-Jahandari*, p. 24; Also Lal, *Khaljis*, pp. 237-38.
104 Barani, pp. 115-116, 328.
105 *Adab-ul Harb* fol. 110a; Barani, p. 327; *Fatawa-i-Jahandari*, p. 24.
106 Afif, p. 290. Also Padmanabha's *Kānhaḍade-prabandha*, pp. 37-38.
107 Barani, p. 328.
108 Afif, p. 88.
109 Barani, p. 253; Ibn Battuta, p. 86; Afif, pp. 224-25; Yahiya, p. 76.

uncertainty of reaching home safely,[110] and the deployment of troops in the battlefield.[111]

Army career held promise of unlimited rise. Avenues of getting promotion and prospects of receiving recognition were always open. Apart from foreign soldiers who rose to become kings and nobles, Indian Musalmans like Malik Kafur, Khusrau Khan and Khan-i-Jahan Maqbul reached close to the throne, and men like Mallu Khan, Sarang Khan, Muqarrab Khan etc., petty soldiers at the start of career, rose to become great nobles and king-makers. Since the solider was the strong prop of the regime, he was its favoured child.[112] In society he was feared and respected because he performed police duties also.

It is doubtful if a soldier could take his family with him on a campaign.[113] Occasionally even nobles were discouraged from taking women with them.[114] However, army men were sometimes provided facilities for communicating with their families when out on a campaign.[115] If no mishap occurred, the soldier returned home often laden with spoils of war. But if he got disabled, he could only hope for care and protection from his relatives in the joint family system because there was no disability or old age pension. However, as Balban discovered, the ineffectives managed to continue on the rolls of the army by bribes and other kinds of subterfuge. Moreover, since there was no retirement age, an armymen continued to hold his post and pay for life. Firoz Tughlaq realizing the difficulties and helplessness of old age, made the profession of soldiers hereditary.[116]

---

110 Afif, p. 201.

111 Al-Qalqashindi, p. 76.

112 Barani, p.102; *Fatawa-i-Jahandari*, p. 21.

113 That is how Alauddin could punish at Delhi the women and children of the troops which had mutinied at Jalor on their way back from the Gujarat campaign (Barani, p. 253; also Afif, p. 173).

114 When he was planning action against Ain-ul-Mulk Multani, Muhammad Tughlaq ordered that no women should remain with the nobles. As a result no women remained in the camp, not even with the Sultan (Ibn Battuta, p. 106). *Adab-ul-Harb* (fol.47 a) also advises against taking women on expeditions.

115 Firoz Tughlaq provided this facility (Afif, p. 173).

116 Afif., pp. 302-303.

This was good only for the soldier and his family, not for the army.

Terror Tactics

The Muslim army looked impressive. There were contingents of Africans, Afghans, Turks, Persians, Indians and others. "The soldiers had excellent horses, magnificent armour, and a fine costume."[117] A soldier usually carried two swords,[118] besides he had bow and arrows, mace and battle axe. The Muslim soldier was an enthusiastic fighter. Psychologically, he was a soldier of Allah. The word '*Jihad*' had a magic appeal for him. His enthusiasm for war was whetted by religious slogans, promises of rewards and prospects of plunder.[119] Consequently, he exhibited great zeal and practised extreme ruthlessness and cruelty.[120] This cruelty gave the army of the Sultanate superiority over Indian forces because it inspired terror wherever it went. Because of his terror tactics the *Turushka* had become a bogey and everywhere inspired a paralysing fear. The captives were made terror-stricken.

It was a common practice to raise towers of skulls of the killed by piling up their heads in mounds. All captives were bound hand and foot and kept under strict surveillance of armed guards until their spirit was completely broken and they could be made slaves, converted, sold, or made to serve on sundry duties. As Ruben Levy points out, "The Turks have always been amongst the most active of Muslim peoples, and if they are not greatly given to pious exercise, they are bigoted believers in this faith and excellent fighters in its cause."[121] The Afghans were equally ferocious. These and other Central and West Asian soliders of "Allah, the Merciful, the Compassionate", were neither

---

117 *Masalik,* E. D., III, p. 576.

118 H.A.R. Gibb, *Ibn Battutah,* p. 216; Ibn Battuta, p. 108.

119 Afif, p. 201.

120 *Adab-ul-Harb*, 115 a, 158 b. After the massacre in Bengal, even Sultan Firoz Tughlaq had begun to weep (Afif, p. 121).

121 *Social Structure of Islam,* op. cit., p. 25.

merciful nor compassionate and created consternation whenever they launched an attack. Balban in the thirteenth century held the conviction that no king could succeed against the army of Delhi, be he a Hindu Raja or a Rana (*mi danam ki pesh lashkar-i-dihli hech badshahi dast ast natawaned kard fikef rayan wa raygan-i-hinduan*).[122]

With the help of the army Muslim rule had spread in most parts of the country and the impression created by it was the same everywhere. A graphic description of Muslim army has been given by the famous fifteenth century Maithili poet, Vidyapati. He had graced the courts of several kings of Tirhut including Shiva Simha, the most well known of them all. After the distingegration of the Delhi. Sultanate at the beginning of the fifteenth century two Muslim kingdoms rose in the East, Bengal and Jaunpur. Shiva Simha's kingdom of Tirhut (Darbhanga region) was sandwiched between the two. There were occasional conflicts in this region between the Tirhut army and those of Bengal and Jaunpur and even Delhi. This is what Vidyapati has to say about the Muslim armies of the neighbouring kingdoms in the fifteenth century. "Sometimes they eat only raw flesh. Their eyes were red with the intoxication of wine. They could run twenty *yojanas* within the span of half of a day. They used to pass the day with the (bare) loaf under their arm... (The soldier) takes into custody all the women of the enemy's city.... Wherever they happened to pass in that very place the ladies of the Raja's house began to be sold in the market. They used to set fire to the villages. They turned out the women (from their homes) and killed the children. Loot was their (source of) income. They subsisted on that. They thrived on injustice and earned fame from war (*kshaya*). Neither did they have pity for the weak nor did they fear the strong...They had nothing to do with righteousness. They never kept their promise... They were neither desirous of good name nor did they fear bad name... It appears on seeing the Turks that they would swallow up the whole lot of Hindus."

122 Barani, p. 52.

Vidyapati wrote in the north-eastern region of Bihar bordering on Nepal. At the other end of the country, the Western part of Rajasthan, Padmanabh, a contemporary of Vidyapti, wrote his famous work *Kānhaḍade-prabandha* in 1455. This epic was written at the instance of Akhairaja, the Chauhan ruler of Jalor, and describes the suffering of the Hindus at the hands of the Muslim army during the invasion of Gujarat by the forces of Alauddin Khilji (1299 CE). In the Sorath (Saurashtra) region, writes Padmanabh, "they made people captive — Brahmanas and children, and women, in fact, people of all (description)... huddled them and tied them by straps of raw hide. The number of prisoners made by them was beyond counting. The prisoners' quarters *(bandikhana)* were entrusted to the care of the Turks." The prisoners suffered greatly and wept aloud. "During the day they bore the heat of the scorching sun, without shade or shelter as they were [in the sandy desert region of Rajasthan], and the shivering cold during the night under the open sky. Children, torn away from their mothers' breasts and homes, were crying. Each one of the captives seemed as miserable as the other. Already writhing in agony due to thirst, the pangs of hunger... added to their distress. Some of the captives were sick, some unable to sit up. Some had no shoes to put on and no clothes to wear. ...Some had iron shackles on their feet. Separated from each other, they were huddled together and tied with straps of hide. Children were separated from their parents, the wives from their husbands, thrown apart by this cruel raid. Young and old were seen writhing in agony, as loud wailings arose from that part of the camp where they were all huddled up... Fercious looking Habshis, quiver-bearers and warriors with battle axes, were also there in the army. The earth shook as this vast army set out...as if sea-tide had swept over the earth and it would wash off everything."[123]

A point to note about these poets is that in contradistinction

123 Vidyapati, *Kīrtilatā*, Indian Press, Allahabad, 1923, pp. 42-44, 70-72; Padmanabh in *Kānhaḍade-prabandha*, op.cit., pp. 11, 16, 18, 38.

to Muslim chroniclers who shower abuses on Hindu kings and people, they bear no ill will towards Muslim invaders. Padmanabh ends his narrative not on a note of hatred for the Turks but that of love for all. "May love and good feelings thrive and blossom amongst all people, nice and gentle. May the hopes and desires of all be fulfilled." Similar is the case with Vidyapati. He even dedicated a poetic composition of his to Sultan Nasir Shah and spoke with admiration of Sultan Ghiyasuddin of Bengal.[124]

Even so their graphic descriptions show how awe-inspiring the army of the Delhi Sultanate was. The gleeful and repeated narratives by Persian chroniclers of the massacres of the people after a battle, loot and plunder and making of captives and converts *(takht-o-taraj)* support these descriptions.

However, cruelty and ruthlessness by themselves do not make a force superior. Therefore, to categorically declare it superior to the Rajput army (again a generic terms for the army of the Hindu rulers in various parts of the country) may not be fair. Comparison between the two would also not be scientifically correct because while much is recorded by chroniclers about the Muslim army of the Sultanate, little is known in detail about that of the Rajputs. If Muhammad Ghauri won the Second Battle of Tarori, Prithviraj defeated him in the first. The Turks captured many important cities in northern India in surprise raids, but local resistance continued and hundreds of Hindu inscriptions claim victories for their kings. Battles between Muslim invaders from Delhi on the one hand and Rajput defenders on the other were always very hotly contested.

For the Muslim army the going was tough form the very beginning; otherwise Fakhr-i-Mudabbir would not have declared that "peace is better than war",[125] and "as far as possible war should be

124 Padmanabh, *Kānhaḍade Prabandha,* trs. Bhatnagar, Canto IV, Verse. 352 cited in introduction, pp. VII-VIII; *The Delhi Sultanate,* Bharatiya Vidya Bhavan, pp. 404-406; Tara Chand, *Influence of Islam on Indian Culture*, p. 214.

125 *Adab-ul-Harb,* fol. 111a.

avoided because it is bitter fare".[126] Such statements from one who, while describing five types of warfare, considers war with the *kafirs* as the most righteous,[127] are not without significance.

Afterword

One reason for enthusiasm for war with *kafirs* was that as the central authority passed into the hands of the Turks and Afghans, the resources of "reduced" Hindu kingdoms went on shrinking over decades and centuries. The mild tax system and the meagre revenue of these small kingdoms precluded the building up, maintenance and efficient working of any large armies. Still, if the Muslim army was on strong grounds on cavalry, the Hindus were equally good if not better in sword, lance and bow. There was no question of total war in those days, and on the field of battle the number of Indian warriors — Kshatriyas and other forward and backward classes — was always larger than that of the invaders. If the Muslims had efficacious engines of war, the Hindus, besides superiority in numbers, possessed a reckless attitude towards life — they were ever ready to lay down their lives on the field of battle. They also gained from some inherent weaknesses of the Muslim army.

In fact, the army of the Sultanate suffered from a number of weaknesses. One was its heterogeneous character. Sometimes troops of the various racial groups could not pull together well or be equally loyal to the regime.[128] Recruitment to the army of the Sultanate continued both from within India and Muslim lands abroad. There were many racial groups, and sometimes many conflicting interests.[129] Ethnic and racial tensions and jealousies were rampant in the Sultanate's army. Slaves, for instance, made good soldiers but (if) "they are of one group and one mind, and there can be no permanent security against their revolt".[130] The

126 Ibid., fols. 66 a-b.
127 Ibid., fols. 131 a-132a
128 Fakfhr-i-Mudabbir, *Tarikh-i-Fakhruddin Mubarak Shah*, pp. 31-32.
129 Afif, p. 223; Al-Qalqashindi, p. 66.
130 Barani, *Fatawa-i-Jahandari*, pp. 25-26.

Afghans had been freely employed by Muhammad Ghauri, Iltutmish, Balban, the Khaljis and the Tughlaqs. Under the Saiyyads and Lodis the whole complexion of the army was changed from "Turk" to "Afghan". The Afghans were brave, sometimes even reckless. But they lacked discipline and were difficult of control. They had a traditional devotion to their own clan leaders — and their clans were many. All this was not conducive to discipline in the army. Armymen could easily shift their loyalties, more so because there was no law of succession to the throne.

Another weakness was that soldiers were habituated to plundering even in peace times. In war, loot for the Musalmans was sanctioned by Islamic scriptures.[131] but when there was no war the soldiers were enjoined to behave with the civilians and not to loot or destroy their property.[132] The massacre of the people of Delhi by Amir Timur was a direct consequence of his soldiers' misbehavior with the market people.[133] The phenomenon repeated itself during Nadir Shah's invasion. As a result sometimes the rowdyism of the armymen brought discredit to the regime. Again, keeping a very large army on a permanent basis had to be ruled out for reasons of finance, security and convenience, and a large portion of the army of the Sultanate remained temporary with loot as its only source of income. Alauddin's keeping an army of about five hundred thousand made him resort to collecting fifty percent of the produce as land revenue even when the imperial resources were large and gains of loot and tribute from his conquests were immense. Other rulers were not financially so sound. The army, besides, could not all be stationed at Delhi; it was distributed all over the Sultanate under provisional governors and garrison commanders.[134] And they could make use of it against the regime itself if they chose to revolt.

Thus the weaknesses in the army of the Sultanate were

131 *Adab-ul-Harb*, fol. 154 b.
132 Ibid., fol. 117 a.
133 Sharafuddin Yazdi, *Zafar Nama*, p. 186; *Zafar-ul-Walih*, III, p. 907.
134 Al-Qalqashindi, pp. 66-67. Also Ibn Battuta, p. 26.

many. But since it won most of the battles and occupied the whole of the northern India in the thirteenth century and penetrated into the South in the fourteenth, its superiority must be acknowledged. This superiority consisted in a system of recruitment and training which turned out excellent human combat material. Evidence about any similar training amongst the Rajputs and warriors belonging to other Hindu castes has yet to be found. Another reason for its having an edge over that of the local rulers was the constant and unbroken arrival of foreign troops like Turks and Afghans. Rajputs could not replenish their manpower from a similar source. That is why if and when the contact of the Delhi Sultans with Muslim homeland was partially or wholly lost (as for example because of the Mongol upheaval in Central Asia), the Rajput princes could contain Turkish expansion in India as the history of the Mamluke Dynasty shows. The Ghazni element was peculiar to the Muslim army. While its cupidity resulted in too much cruelty in warfare, it added a very zealous element to the fighting forces. Islam gave them a unity of thought, interest and action. Their terror-tactics and acts of cruelty struck awe in the hearts of its victims and helped in the extension of Muslim rule. It is no mean achievement, therefore, that the country could preserve its religion and culture in spite of persistent onslaughts. India is one country which saved itself from becoming Islamic in the medieval period; this could be possible because of the sacrifices of all sections of society — high castes and low castes, forward classes and backward classes, Savarnas and Dalits.

Bibliography

Original Sources

Abbas Sarwani, see Sarwani.

Abdullah, *Tarikh-i-Daudi,* Bankipore Ms. Text, ed. by S.A. Rashid, Aligarh, 1954.

Abdullah Wassaf, see Wassaf.

Abul Fazl, Allami, *Ain-i-Akbari,* 3 vols., Vol.I trs. by H. Blochmann and ed. by D.C. Phillot, Calcutta, 1939; Vol.II trs. by H.S. Jarret and annotated by Jadunath Sarkar, Calcutta, 1939; Vol.III trs. by Jarret and Sarkar, Calcutta, 1948.

Abul Fazl, Allami, *Akbar Nama,* Bib. Ind. Text, 3 vols., English trs. by Henry Beveridge, Calcutta, 1948.

Afif, Shams Siraj, *Tarikh-i-Firoz Shahi,* Bib. Ind., Calcutta, 1890.

Ahmad Yadgar, *Tarikh-i-Salatin-i-Afghana,* Bib. Ind., Calcutta, 1936.

Alberuni, Abu Raihan Muhammad., *Alberuni's India,* Eng. trs. by Edward Sachau, 2 vols., London, 1910.

Al Biladuri, *Futuh-ul-Buldan* (written 9th cent. C.E.), trs. in E.D., vol.I.

Al Kufi, *Chach Nama,* trs. in E and D, I. Also by Mirza Kalichbeg Fredunbeg, Karachi, 1900, Delhi reprint, 1979.

Al Qalqashindi, *Subh-ul-Asha,* trs. by Otto Spies as *An Arab Account of India in the 14th Century*, Aligarh, 1935.

Al Umri, see Shihabuddin.

Amir Khusrau, Abul Hasan, *Deval Rani,* Aligarh, 1917.

Amir Khusrau, Abul Hasan, *Tughlaq Nama,* ed. by Hashim Faridabadi, Aurangabad, 1933.

Amir Khusrau, Abul Hasan, *Nuh Sipihr,* ed. Muhammad Wahid Mirza, O.U.P. Calcutta, 1948.

Amir Khusrau, Abul Hasan, *Khazain-ul-Futuh,* ed. M.W. Mirza (Calcutta 1953). English trs. by Mohammad Habib entitled Campaigns of Alauddin Khilji, Madras, 1931.

Babur, Zahiruddin Muhammad, *Babur Nama or Tuzuk-i-Baburi,* trs. from Turki by Mrs. A.S. Beveridge, 2 vols., London, 1922; trs. from the Persian version by John Leyden and William Erskine as *Memoirs of Babur,* London, 1926.

Badaoni, Abdul Qadir Ibn-i-Muluk Shah, *Muntakhab-ut-Tawarikh,* ed. by Ahmad Ali, Persian Text, Bib. Ind., 3 vols., Calcutta, 1864-67; English trs. by George S.A. Ranking, Calcutta, 1898.

Barani, Ziyauddin, *Tarikh-i-Firoz Shahi,* Bib. Ind., Calcutta, 1864.

Barani, Ziyauddin, *Fatawa-i-Jahandari,* English trs. by Afsar Begum and Mohammad Habib, Allahabad, 1960.

Barani, Ziyauddin, *Sana-i-Muhammadi,* trs. in *Medieval India Quarterly,* vol.I, pt.III.

Bihamad Khani, Muhammad, *Tarikh-i-Muhammadi,* British Museum Ms.; Rotograph copy in Allahabad University Library; English trs. by Muhammad Zaki, Aligarh, 1972.

Dargah Quli Khan, *Muraqqa-i-Dihli,* Persian Text and Urdu trs. by Nurul Hasan Ansari, Delhi, 1982.

Fakhr-i-Mudabbir, *Tarikh-i-Fakhruddin Mubarak Shah,* ed. by Sir Denison Ross, London, 1927.

Fakhr-i-Mudabbir, *Adabul Harb wa Shujaat,* Photocopy British Museum, Add. 1653; Hindi trs. in Rizvi, *Adi Turk Kalin* Bharat.

Farid Bhakkari, *Zakhirat-ul-Khawanin,* Karachi, 1961.

Farishtah, Muhammad Qasim Hindu Shah, *Gulshan-i-Ibrahimi,* also known as *Tarikh-i-Farishtah,* Persian Text, Lucknow, 1865.

Gulbadan Begum, *Humayun Nama,*Persian text and Eng. trs. by A.S. Beveridge, 1910, Delhi Reprint, 1972.

Hajiuddabir, *Zafar-ul-Wali bi Muzaffar Wali, An Arabic History of Gujarat,* ed. by Sir Denison Ross, 3 vols., London, 1910, 1921.

Hasan Nizami, *Taj-ul-Maasir,* trs. by S.H. Askari in *Patna University Journal* (Arts), vol.18, No.3, 1963; also in E.D. II.

Hidaya Kitab al Siyar wail Jihad Mujtabai Press, Delhi, 2 vols., 1331, 1332 H. Also see Hamilton under Modern Works.

Ibn Battuta, *The Rehla of Ibn Battuta,* English trs. by Dr. Agha Mahdi Husain, Oriental Institute, Broda, 1953; French trs. as *Ibn Batoutahs Voyages* by C. Defremery and B.R. Sanguinetti, Paris, 1857. Hindi trs. by S.A.A. Rizvi in Tughlaq Kalin Bharat, 1956-57.

Isami, Khwaja Abdulla Malik, *Futuh-us-Salatin,* ed. by Agha Mahdi

Husain, Educational Press, Agra, 1938.

Jahangir, Nuruddin Muhammad, *Tuzuk-i-Jahangiri* or *Memoirs of Emperor Jahangir*, trs. by Rogers and Beveridge, Delhi Reprint, 1968. See also Price for *Tarikh-i-Salim Shahi*.

Jaisi, Malik Muhammad, *Padmavat*, ed. by R.C. Shukla, Allahabad, 1935.

Jauhar, *Tazkirat-ul-Waqiat*, trs. by C. Stewart, 1832, Indian reprint, 1972.

Khafi Khan, Muhammad Hashim, *Muntakhab-ul-Lubab*, ed. by Kabir-ud-din Ahmad, Bib.Ind., Calcutta, 1869, 1925.

Minhaj Siraj Jurjani, *Tabqat-i-Nasiri*, Bib. Ind., Calcutta, 1864; English trs. by Major H.R. Raverty, London, 1881.

Mir Khwand, *Rauzat-us-Safa*, Bombay 1271 H.

Niamatullah, *Makhzan-i-Afghana*, trs. by Nirodbhushan Roy as *History of the Afghans*, Santiniketan, 1958; also B. Dorn's trs., 2 parts, London, 1829-36.

Nizamuddin Ahmad, *Tabqat-i-Akbari*, Bib. Ind., 3 vols., Calcutta, 1927-35; also trs. by B. De.

Padmanabh, *Kanhadade Prabandh*, translated and annotated by V.S. Bhatnagar, New Delhi, 1991.

Price, Major David, *Tarikh-i-Salim Shahi*, trs. under the title of *Memoirs of the Emperor Jahanguer, written by himself*, London, 1829; Indian edition, Calcutta, 1906. Also see Price under Modern Works.

Ranking, see Badaoni.

Reynolds, see Utbi

Rizqullah Mushtaqi, *Waqiat-i-Mushtaqi*, Photo copy of the British Museum Ms. Ad. 11633.

Sarwani, Abbas, *Tarikh-i-Sher Shahi*, trs. in E.D., IV.

Shihabuddin al Umri, *Masalik-ul-Absar fi Mumalik-ul-Amsar* (written in middle of 14th cent. C.E.), trs. in E.D., III; Hindi trs. in Rizvi,

Tughlaq Kalin Bharat.

Timur, Amir, *Malfuzat-i-Timuri,* trs. in E.D., III.

Utbi, Abu Nasr Muhammad, *Kitab-i-Yamini,* trs. by James Reynolds, London, 1858; also in E.D., II.

Vidyapati, *Kirtilata,* Allahabad, 1923.

Wassaf, Abdullah, *Tajziat-ul-Amsar wa Tajriyat-ul-Asar,* also called *Tarikh-i-Wassaf* (written 1327 C.E.), Bombay, 1877.

Yahiya Sarhindi, *Tarikh-i-Mubarak Shahi,* Bib. Ind. Text edited by M. Hidayat Husain, Calcutta, 1931; English trs. by K.K. Basu, Baroda, 1932.

Yazdi, Sharafuddin, *Zafar Nama,* 2 vols., Bib. Ind., Calcutta, 1885-88.

Ziyauddin Barani, see Barani.

Foreign Travellers' Accounts

Barbosa, Duarte, *The Book of Duarte Barbosa,* 2 vols., London, 1918-21.

Bernier, Francois, *Travels in the Mogul Empire* (1656-1668), revised by V.A. Smith, Oxford, 1934.

De Laet, John, *The Empire of the Great Mogol,* trs. by Hoyland and Banerjee, Bombay, 1928.

Della Valle, *The Travels of Pietro Della Valle in India,* trs. by Edward Grey, 2 vols., London, 1892.

Finch, William, see Foster

Foster, William, *Early Travels in India* (1583-1619), contains narratives of Fitch (pp.1-47), Mildenhall (pp.48-59), Hawkins (pp.60-121), Finch (pp.122-87), Withington (pp.188-233), Coryat (pp.234-87) and Terry (pp.288-322), London, 1927.

Ibn Battuta, see under Original Sources.

Major, R.H., *India in the Fifteenth Century,* contains extracts from narratives of Nicolo Conti, Santo Stefano, etc., London, 1857.

Manrique, *Travels of Frey Sebastian Manrique,* trs. by Eckford Luard, 2 vols., London, 1927.

Manucci, Niccolao, *Storia do Mogor,* trs. by W. Irvine, 4 vols., London, 1906.

Marco Polo, see Yule

Mundy, Peter, *Travels of Peter Mundy in Asia,* ed. by R.C. Temple, London, 1914.

Pelsaert, Francisco, *Jahangir's India,* trs. by W.H. Moreland and P. Geyl, Cambridge, 1925.

Tavernier, *Travels in India,* trs. and ed. by V. Ball, London, 1925.

Terry, Edward, A *Voyage to East India,* London, 1655.

Thevenot, *Indian Travels of Thevenot and Careri,* ed. by Surendra Nath Sen, New Delhi, 1949.

Varthema, *The Itinerary of Ludovico di Varthema of Bologna,* ed. by Sir Richard Temple, London, 1928.

Yule, Sir Henry, and H. Cordier, *The Book of Ser Marco Polo,* 2 vols., New York, 1903.

Modern Works

A Gazetteer of Baluchistan, Calcutta 1908, Reprint Vintage Books, Gurgaon, Haryana, 1989.

Aghnides, Nicholas P., *Muhammadan Theories of Finance,* New York, 1916.

Albairuni, A.H., *Makers of Pakistan and Modern Muslim Indians,* Muhammad Ashraf Publishers, Lahore.

Anwar Shaikh, see Shaikh Anwar.

Bengal, 2 vols. Calcutta 1908, Delhi 1984.

Beni Prasad, *A History of Jahangir,* Third ed., Allahabad, 1940.

Bharatiya Vidya Bhavan, see Majumdar, R.C.

Bhatkhande, V.N. A short Historical Survey of the Music of Upper India.

Bosworth, C.E., *The Ghaznavids: Their Empire in Afghanistan and Eastern Iran,* 994-1040, Edinburgh, 1963.

Brown, Percy, *Indian Architecture (Islamic Period),* Third ed., Bombay, n.d.

The Cambridge History of India,
vol.III, ed. by Wolseley Haig, Delhi reprint, 1958.
vol.IV, ed. by Richard Burn, Cambridge, 1937.

Caroe, Sir Olaf, *The Pathans,* Macmillan & Co., London., 1958.

Central India, Calcutta 1908, Delhi 1989.

Chandawat, P.C., *Maharaja Surajmal aur unka Yug* (Hindi), Agra, 1982.

Chaturvedi, Parasuram, *Sant Kavya,* Kitab Mahal, Allahabad, 1952.

Chowdhry, Shiv Rai, *Al Hajjay Ibn Yusuf,* Delhi University Press, 1972.

Crooke, William, *Tribes and Castes of North Western Provinces and Oudh,* Calcutta, 1896.

Dani, Ahmad Hasan, "Race and Culture Complexin Bengal," in *Social Research in East Pakistan,* Ed. P. Bessaignet, Asiatic Society of Pakistan, Dacca, 1960.

Digby, Simon, *War Horse and Elephant in the Delhi Sultanate,* Oxford, 1971.

Dikshitar, V.R.R., *War in Ancient India,* second edition, Macmillan & Co., 1948.

Dorn, Benhard, *History of the Afghans,* being trs. of *Makhzan-i-Afghana,* London, 1829.

Duff, Grant, J.C., *History of the Marathas,* Bombay, 1878.

Eastern Bengal and Assam, Calcutta 1909, Delhi, 1989.

Eaton, Richard Maxwell, *Sufis of Bijapur* (1300-1700), Princeton, 1978.

Elliot, H.M. and J. Dowson, *History of India as told by its own Historians,* 8 vols, London, 1867-77; vol.II, Aligarh reprint, 1952.

Elst, Koenraad, *Indigenous Indians: Agastya to Ambedkar,* Voice of India, New Delhi, 1993.

Encyclopaedia Britannica

Encyclopaedia of Islam, Luzac & Co., 1913-38.

Epigraphia Indica, Arabic and Persian Supplement, 1956-60.

Frawley, David, *Hinduism the Eternal Tradition,* New Delhi, 1995.

Frawley, David, *Arise Arjuna, Hinduism and the Modern World,* Voice of India, New Delhi, 1995.

Gaur, R.C. "Medieval Roads and Shops in Fatehpur Sikri," Proceedings Indian History Congress, 1982.

Gautier, Francis, *The Wonder that is India,* Voice of India, New Delhi, 1994.

Gazetteers of Alwar, Trubner & Co., London, 1878.

Gazetteer of Afghanistan Calcutta 1908, Reprint Vintage Books Gurgaon, 1989.

Gazetteer of Afghanistan and Nepal, Calcutta 1908. Reprint Vintage Books Gurgaon, 1989.

Gupta, Satya Prakash, *The Agrarian System of Eastern Rajasthan* (1650-1750) Manohar, Delhi, 1986.

Habib, Mohammad, *Sultan Mahmud of Ghaznin,* Delhi reprint, 1951.

Habib, Mohammad, *Some Aspects of the Foundation of the Delhi Sultanate,* K.M. Ashraf Memorial Lecture, Delhi, 1966.

Habib, Mohammad, *Compaigns of Alauddin Khilji,* being trs. of Amir Khusrau's *Khazain-ul-Futuh,* Bombay, 1933.

Habib, Mohammad, Introduction to E and D, II, Aligarh, 1951.

Habib, Mohammad, *Collected Works,* entitled *Politics and Society During Early Medieval Period,* edited by K.A. Nizami, vol.I, 1974; vol.II, 1981.

Habibullah, A.B.M., *The Foundation of Muslim Rule in India,* Revised ed., Allahabad, 1961, first published, Lahore, 1945.

Hamilton, Charles, trs., *Hedayah,* 4 vols., London, 1791.

Harihar Niwas Dwivedi, *Man Singh aur Man Kutuhal* (Hindi).

Hasan, Mohibbul Hasan, *Kashmir under the Sultans,* Iran Soviety, Calcutta, 1959.

Hodivala, S.H., *Studies in Indo-Muslim History,* Bombay, 1939.

Hughes, T.P., *Dictionary of Islam,* W.H. Allen & Co., London, 1885, *Bombay Presidency*, 2 vols. Calcutta 1909, Delhi 1985.

Hyderabad State, Calcutta 1909, Delhi 1989.

Imperial Gazetteer of India, Provincial Series, Superintendent of Printing, Calcutta 1908, 1909, Reprinted Usha Jain Daryaganj, New Delhi, 1984, 1989.

India 1993, Publications Division, Government of India, January, 1994.

Indian Antiquary.

Indian Historical Quarterly.

Indian History Congress, Proceedings.

Ira Marvin Lapidus, *Muslim Cities in the Later Middle Ages*, Cambridge, Mass., 1967.

Irvine, W., *The Army of the Indian Moghuls*, London, 1903.

Ishwari Prasad, *A History of the Qaraunah Turks in India*, vol.I, Allahabad, 1936.

Ishwari Prasad, *History of Medieval India*, Fourth impression, Allahabad, 1940.

Islamic Culture, Hyderabad.

Journal of the (Royal) Asiatic Society of Bengal.

Kane, P.V., *History of Dharmashastra*, 5 vols., Bhandarkar Oriental Research Institute, Poona, 1946-1968.

Kennedy, Pringle, *A History of the Great Mughals*, Calcutta, 1905, 1911.

Khan, Refaqat Ali, *The Kachhwahas under Akbar and Jahangir*, Jamia Millia Islamia, 1976.

Abdul Majid, "Research about Muslim Aristocracy in East Pakistan" in Pierre Bessaignet (ed.) *Social Research in East Pakistan*, Dacca, 1960.

Khan, M.S., "The Life and Works of Fakhre Mudabbir" in *Islamic Culture*, April, 1977.

Kolf, Dirk H.A., *Naukar, Rajput and Sepoy: the ethnohistory of the military labour market in Hindustan* (1450-1850), Cambridge University Press, 1990.

Lal, K.S., *History of the Khaljis*, New Delhi, 1980, first published 1950.

Lal, K.S., *Twilight of the Sultanate*, New Delhi, 1980, first published, 1963.

Lal, K.S., *Studies in Medieval Indian History*, Ranjit Publshers, Delhi, 1966.

Lal, K.S., *Growth of Muslim Population in Medieval India*, Research Publications in Social Sciences,New Delhi, 1973.

Lal, K.S., *The Mughal Harem,* Aditya Prakashan, New Delhi, 1988.

Lal, K.S., *Indian Muslims: Who Are They,* Voice of India, New Delhi, 1990.

Lal, K.S. *Muslim Slave System in Medieval India,* New Delhi, 1994.

Lal, K.S., 'The Ghaznavids in India', in *Bengal Past and Present,* Sir Jadunath Sarkar Birth Centenary Number, July-December, 1970.

Lal, K.S., 'Striking Power of the Army of the Sultanate' in the *Journal of Indian History,* Vol. LV, Pt. III, December, 1977.

Lapidus, see Ira Marvin.

Levy, Ruben, *The Social Structure of Islam,* Cambridge, 1962.

Madras, 2 vols. Calcutta 1908, Delhi 1985.

Mahdi Husain, *Tughlaq Dynasty,* Thacker Spink & Co. Calcutta, 1963.

Mahdi Husain, *Shah Namah-i-Hind* or trs. of Isami's *Futuh-us-Salatin,* 3 vols., Aligarh, 1976-77.

Majumdar, R.C. (ed.), *The Delhi Sultanate,* Bombay, 1960.

Mazumdar, B.P., *The Socio-Economic History of Northern India* (1030-1194 A.D.), Calcutta, 1960.

Mishra, Suresh, *Garha ke Gond Rajya ka utthan aur patan* (Hindi), Rani Durgavati Vishwavidyalaya, Jabalpur, 1986.

Mitra, R.C., *The Decline of Buddhism in India,* Visvabharati, 1954.

Moreland, W.H., *India at the Death of Akbar,* Macmillan, London, 1920.

Moreland, W.H., *From Akbar to Aurangzeb,* London, 1923.

Moreland, W.H., *The Agrarian System of Moslem India,* London, 1929.

Muhammad Aziz Ahmad, *Political History and Institutions of the Early Turkish Empire of Delhi* (1206-1290 A.D.), New Delhi, 1949, 1972.

Muhammad Shaban, *Islamic History* II (750-1055) Cambridge University Press, 1958.

Munshi, K.M., 'End of Ancient India' in Bharatiya Vidya Bhavan Journal, December, 1959.

Mysore and Coorg, Calcutta 1908, Delhi 1985.

Naqvi, Hamida Khatoon, *Urbanisation and Urban Centres under the Great Mughals,* 1556-1707, Simla, 1971.

Naqvi, Hamida Khatoon, *Agricultural, Industrial and Urban Dynamics under the Sultans of Delhi,* New Delhi, 1986.

Prasad, Rajiv Nain, *Raja Man Singh of Amber*, Calcutta, 1966.

Price, Major David, *Memoirs of the Principal Events of Muhammadan History*, 3 vols., London, 1921. Also see Price under Original Sources.

Provincial Gazetteers of Kashmir and Jammu, by Walter R. Lawrence, Reprint Prima Publishing House, Inderpuri, New Delhi, 1985.

Punjab, 2 vols., Calcutta 1908, Delhi 1984.

Rajputana, Calcutta 1908, Delhi 1989.

Ram Swarup, *Anusmiriti and Anudhyāyana*.

Risley, H.H. *The Tribes and Castes of Bengal*, Bengal Secretariat Press, Calcutta, 1891.

Rizvi, Saiyyad Athar Abbas, *Muslim Revivalist Movements in North India in the Sixteenth and Seventeenth Centuries*, Agra University, Agra, 1965.

Rizvi, Saiyyad Athar Abbas, *A History of Sufism in India*, 2 Vols., 1978, 1983.

Rizvi, Saiyyad Athar Abbas, *Adi Turk Kalin Bharat*, Aligarh, 1965.

Rizvi, Saiyyad Athar Abbas, *Tughlaq Kalin Bharat*, 2 parts, 1956, 1957.

Rizvi, Saiyyad Athar Abbas, *Uttar Timur Kalin Bharat*, Part II, Aligarh, 1959.

Saksena, Banarsi Prasad, *History of Shahjahan of Dehli*, Second Impression, Allahabad, 1961.

Saran, Parmatma, *Resistance of Indian Princess to Turkish Offensive*, Sita Ram Kohli Memorial Lectures, Punjabi University, Patiala, 1967.

Sarkar, Jadunath, *History of Aurangzeb*, 5 vols., Calcutta, 1912-25.

Sarkar, Jadunath, *A Short History of Aurangzeb*, Calcutta, 1930.

Sarkar, Jadunath, *Shivaji and his Times* 4th ed. Calcutta, 1948.

Sewell, Robert, *A Forgotten Empire* (Vijayanagar), New Delhi reprint, 1966.

Shaban, see Muhammad Shaban.

Shaikh, Anwar, in *Liberty*, Humanist Quarterly. Principality Publishers, 4-6 Llantrisant Street, Cardiff, U.K.

Sharma, Gopi Nath, *Mewar and the Mughal Emperors*, Agra, 1954.

Sharma, Suresh, *Tribal Identity and the Modern World*, Sage Publishers,

New Delhi.

Siddiqi, Iqtidar Husain, *Some Aspects of Afghan Despotism in India,* Aligarh, 1969.

Singhal, D.P., *India and World Civilization,* 2 vols., Rupa & Co., Delhi, 1972.

Smith, V.A., *Akbar the Great Mogul,* Delhi reprint, S. Chand & Co., 1962.

Srivastava, A.L., *The Mughal Empire,* Agra, 1964.

Sykes, P.M., *A History of Persia,* 2 vols., Macmillan & Co., London, 1915.

Tara Chand, *History of Freedom Movement in India,* 3 vols., Publications Division, India.

Tara Chand, *Influence of Islam on Indian Culture,* Indian Press, Allahabad, 1946.

The Gazetter of Central Provinces of India, Ed., Sir Charles Grant, 2nd ed., 1870, Delhi, 1984.

Thomas, Edward, *Chronicles of the Pathan Kings of Delhi,* London, 1871.

Tod, James, *Annals and Antiquities of Rajasthan,* Routledge & Kegan Paul, 2 vols., London, 1957.

Toy, Sidney, *The Strongholds of India,* London, 1957.

Tripathi, R.P., *Some Aspects of Muslim Administration,* Allahabad, 1936.

Troise, J., *Tribal Religion,* South Asia Books, Manohar, Delhi, 1978.

United Provinces of Agra and Oudh, 2 vols, Calcutta 1908, Delhi, 1984.

Venkataramanayya, N., *The Early Muslim Expansion in South India,* Madras University, 1942.

Westcott, *Kabir and Kabir Panth,* Cawnpore, 1907.

Will and Ariel Durant, *The Lessons of History,* Simon and Schuster, New York, 1968.

Wink, Andre, *Al-Hind: The Making of the Indo-Islamic World,* vol.I, *Early Medieval India,* Oxford University Press, Delhi, 1990.

Index